CONGRESS
AT WAR

Library of Congress Cataloging-in-Publication Data

Softcover ISBN 978-1-59797-181-2

(alk. paper)

Printed in the United States of America on acid-free paper that meets the American National Standards Institute Z39-48 Standard.

Available from:

Potomac Books, Inc.
22841 Quicksilver Drive
Dulles, Virginia 20166
800-775-2518

2007 Edition

10 9 8 7 6 5 4 3 2

CONGRESS AT WAR

The Politics of Conflict Since 1789

CHARLES A. STEVENSON

NDU Press

National Defense University Press
Washington, DC

Potomac Books, Inc.
Washington, DC

CONTENTS

Illustrations

CHAPTER 1

INTRODUCTION

> If we cannot inquire into the state of the Army, it follows that the Army belongs to the President and not to the nation.
> —*Nathaniel Macon*
> *(D–NC, three-term Speaker of the House), 1810*[1]

> I have much doubted whether, in case of a war, Congress would find it practicable to do their part of the business. That a body containing 100 lawyers in it, should direct the measures of a war is, I fear, impossible.
> —*Thomas Jefferson to President James Madison,*
> *February 19, 1812*[2]

What is the proper congressional role in the conduct of major military operations? There has been considerable controversy over this issue in recent years. Most of the debate has been over the initiation of combat. Presidentialists argue that the President's executive authority permits him to act to defend the Nation's interests whether or not Congress has acted. In an age of nuclear weapons and terrorism, they contend, the need for urgent action, perhaps even preemption, supersedes the 18th-century notions embedded in the Constitution.

Constitutional purists argue that the power to declare war is equivalent to the power to authorize the commencement of hostile military operations except in response to an invasion or insurrection and that prior authorization is required in almost all cases when U.S. forces are sent into harm's way. Some in Congress found the War Powers Resolution defective precisely because it allowed the President to send troops into combat for 60 days without prior authorization.

Whatever lawyers may argue, the historical record shows that some Presidents have initiated the use of force without suffering congressional sanctions, and some Congresses have acted successfully to restrain Commanders in Chief. John Yoo, a legal scholar and a strong Presidentialist, has nevertheless concluded that the founding generation of American leaders devised "a flexible system for making foreign policy in which the political branches could opt to cooperate or compete. The constitution did not intend to institute a fixed, legalistic process for the making of war or treaties. On the question of war, flexibility means there is no one constitutionally correct method for waging war."[3]

Since this study goes beyond the initiation of hostilities to review congressional roles in the conduct, oversight, and termination of major military operations, it runs into another body of opinion that sees a solid firewall between the legislative branch and the men at arms. Presidentialists subscribe to the "unitary executive" school of thought that argues that the President must be unfettered in his performance of key executive functions, particularly defense and warmaking. As Department of Justice lawyers argued in formal legal memoranda after the 9/11 attacks, "The President enjoys complete discretion in the exercise of his Commander-in-Chief authority and in conducting operations against hostile forces."[4]

Other Presidentialist legal scholars have amplified this point. "What Congress cannot do, however, is direct how a President prosecutes a particular war—including decisions about how many of the available forces to introduce into a theater of conflict."[5] Or this: "Only Congress could create an army, but once one was established, it was within the President's constitutional discretion to determine how it was to be deployed, with the sole exception that he could not declare war." This latter scholar even argues that "in foreign affairs, with respect to the powers vested directly and exclusively in the President by the American people through the Constitution, Congress may not seize control of those powers by placing conditions on appropriations."[6]

The trouble with these arguments, however strongly felt and meticulously argued, is that the historical record demonstrates that neither all Congresses nor all Presidents have accepted their validity. Some Congresses have tried to direct aspects of the conduct of war and have written restrictive language into appropriations, and Presidents have sometimes complied. For example, lawmakers refused to approve certain authorities and/or military capabilities specifically requested by nine Presidents: George Washington, John Adams, James Madison, James Polk, William McKinley, Woodrow Wilson, Franklin Roosevelt, Lyndon Johnson, and George W. Bush (see table 1–1). Congress has also imposed legally binding restrictions on the use of force that were accepted by seven Presidents: McKinley, Franklin Roosevelt, Richard Nixon, Gerald Ford, Ronald Reagan, William Clinton, and George W. Bush

Table 1–1. Presidential Military Requests Denied by Congress

President	Request	Year
George Washington	Militia rules and support	1792
John Adams	Stronger Navy, coastal fortifications, artillery	1797
James Madison	Conscription; declaration of war on Algiers	1813–1814; 1815
James Polk	Larger Army, lieutenant general rank, $2 million peace fund	1846–1847
William McKinley	Increase Regular Army, limit volunteers	1898
Woodrow Wilson	Arm merchantmen	1917
Franklin Roosevelt	Labor draft	1944
Lyndon Johnson	Draft lottery	1967
George W. Bush	Blanket authority to deter and prevent terrorism	2001

Table 1–2. Congressional Restrictions Accepted by Presidents

President	Restriction	Year
William McKinley	No annexation of Cuba	1898
Franklin Roosevelt	No arms sales to belligerents; no transfers of needed U.S. arms; no draftees serving outside of Western Hemisphere	1930s; 1940; 1940-1941
Richard Nixon	No ground combat forces into Laos or Thailand; no reintroduction of troops to Cambodia; no combat operations in southeast Asia after August 15, 1973	1969; 1970; 1973
Gerald Ford	No military operations in Angola	1976
Ronald Reagan	Combat in Lebanon restricted to self-defense; no military activities in Nicaragua	1983; 1980s
William Clinton	No troops in Somalia after March 31, 1994; no military actions in Rwanda after October 7, 1994	1993; 1994
George W. Bush	Ceiling on military personnel and contractors in Colombia	2000– present

(see table 1–2). Maybe neither branch should have done these things, but they have; and judges and legal scholars have long believed that precedents create future options.

Presidentialists sometimes criticize these precedents as injurious as well as illegal—and that is more relevant to this study. The focus here is not what lawyers may argue, but what political leaders have done and why. While this study aims to avoid sterile legal debates, it is comforting to note one legal scholar's argument that precedents gain legitimacy when they do not supplant clear constitutional requirements and are systematic and long pursued.[7]

THE HISTORICAL RECORD

This study examines the precedents established over two centuries and reveals more varieties of behavior than is generally recognized. Congress is discriminating in how it authorizes force. Lawmakers have shown both aggressiveness and restraint. They have been willing at times to empower Presidents and at other times to set conditions and limits. They also have taken the initiative. It was Congress, not the President, that pressed hardest for war against Britain in 1812, against Spain in 1898, against Cuba in 1962, and in Bosnia in the 1990s. Other Congresses denied or restricted Presidential warmaking authorities in 1797–1798, 1815, in the years before Pearl Harbor, in Lebanon in 1983, and after the 9/11 attacks. Congress specifically banned certain U.S. combat operations—in Laos and Thailand in 1969, in Angola in 1976, and in Nicaragua in the 1980s. Lawmakers also enacted measures forbidding the reintroduction of troops or continuation of military operations after Presidents had agreed to end their missions.

Congress has also been discriminating in what kinds of forces to build or raise for different conflicts, sometimes favoring a particular Service or technology, sometimes preferring militia to regular forces. Congress was reluctant to build up the Navy in 1798 but did so quite enthusiastically a century later. Lawmakers wanted to rely on the militia for ground forces throughout the 19th century but refused to pass legislation standardizing and supporting militia training and equipment. In the 1980s, Congress imposed a strengthened Special Operations Forces Command on a reluctant Pentagon.

When asked, Congress usually has been willing to increase tariffs and taxes to help pay for conflicts and also to authorize borrowing when those revenues were insufficient. This was the case in all conflicts from the 1790s through the Korean War, except the War of 1812. When not asked by the President to pay for the conflicts by imposing taxes or domestic budgetary restraint,

Congress has been quite willing to avoid painful political choices, as was the case in the War of 1812, Vietnam, and Iraq.

Only rarely has Congress sought directly through legislative actions to influence grand strategy during wartime, but individual members have often weighed in with their recommendations. In the Civil War, Congress tried to force the President to free slaves and recruit former slaves sooner than President Abraham Lincoln was ready to embrace emancipation as a war aim. In the years before Pearl Harbor, Congress imposed tight restrictions on providing arms to belligerents and on sending U.S. draftees outside the Western Hemisphere. In Southeast Asia, Congress prohibited the sending of ground combat forces into Laos and Thailand and then barred their reintroduction into Cambodia. The same kinds of restrictions were later voted for Somalia and Rwanda.

When in session, and when conflicts lasted at least for several months, Congress has undertaken oversight investigations and hearings, most often concentrating on training, equipment, and contracting rather than military strategy. Often, special committees have been established, and they have conducted vigorous oversight, as they did in the Civil War, World War II, Korea, Vietnam, and, to some extent, in Iraq. Lawmakers have investigated atrocity reports in many conflicts, notably the Philippines, Haiti, the Dominican Republic, Korea, Vietnam, and Iraq.

On the other hand, Congress has been inconsistent in asserting its constitutional prerogatives. The legislative branch has become most engaged in critical oversight when wars become lengthy and/or stalemated, as in the two World Wars, Korea, Vietnam, and Iraq. When the wars are short and successful, lawmakers join in the applause. Congress also sought after-action reports from the Presidents in the War of 1812, the Spanish-American War of 1898, and the Gulf War of 1991.

Even major assertions of constitutional prerogatives, such as the War Powers Resolution, are honored more in the breach. The very fact that Congress in recent years has often failed to complete any legislative action—in support, criticism, or direction of major military operations—undercuts its power and authority over future conflicts. Despite debate, votes, and even passage of significant legislation in at least one chamber, Congress failed to send legislation to the President authorizing or guiding military operations in the Philippines or Korea, Panama in 1989, or Haiti, Somalia, Bosnia, or Kosovo in the 1990s. It is also the case that members of the political party opposite that of the President are usually the most vocal regarding the rights of Congress to be involved in decisions to enter conflicts, while the President's partisans tend to be supportive of his policies and more willing to grant him freedom of action. Evaluation of precedents shows some to be restrictive, constraining, interfering, or injurious. Others seem to be either supportive and legitimate or properly intrusive. Together, they provide a menu of examples that can be studied and may be applied in present and future conflicts.

CONSTITUTIONAL BACKGROUND

The Constitution was framed in a process much like the legislative process in Congress. Factions presented differing proposals that protected their parochial interests; votes were taken, and deadlocks were reached; differences were papered over with ambiguous language; and eventually, a compromise document was produced that most, but not all, delegates could accept.

In Philadelphia in 1787, the large states proposed a legislature based on population. The small states wanted equal representation because they knew that the three biggest states—Massachusetts, Pennsylvania, and Virginia—had 45 percent of the population and could dominate the government with the support of only one other state.[8]

The turning point came on July 2, 1787, when a motion for equal representation nearly passed. It failed on a tie vote, showing the strength of sentiment for protection of small states. Soon thereafter, the delegates agreed to the Grand Compromise of a House of Representatives based on population and a Senate with equal votes for each state. This agreement changed the dynamic of the convention because the small states, assured of protection in the Senate, were at last willing to create a strong Federal Government.[9]

Security concerns were a major motivation for calling the convention, both to overcome the weakness of the government under the Articles of Confederation and to prevent foreign powers from threatening the unity of the states by force or bribery. Eleven of the 18 specific powers granted to Congress under the new Constitution related explicitly to security.[10] The delegates were wary of standing armies and determined to keep the warriors under the control of civilian elected officials, so they made the President Commander in Chief and put a 2-year time limit on funds for the Army. They expected state militias to be the source of most soldiers but recognized that the troops might have to be called into Federal service to suppress insurrections and repel invasions and enforce the laws—but only on terms and conditions set by the Congress.[11]

A key debate occurred on August 17, when the delegates discussed language from the Committee on Detail giving Congress the power to "make war." When one delegate argued that Congress acted too slowly, James Madison suggested a change from "make" to "declare" war, saying this would give "the executive the power to repel sudden attacks." Roger Sherman of Connecticut agreed, saying that "the executive should be able to repel and not commence war."[12] Most of the legal debates since then have turned on the difference intended by the change of wording. Authors can cite Madison for a very broad reading of the power of Congress and Alexander Hamilton for a defense of a strong executive.

Despite the changes and compromises made by the delegates, several recognized patriots—George Mason, Patrick Henry, Elbridge Gerry, and James Monroe—refused to sign or support the new Constitution. So great were the concerns about the military provisions of the new document that nearly every state's ratifying convention proposed additional amendments warning against standing armies, further limiting congressional power to raise armies, or forbidding the quartering of soldiers in private homes.[13]

In practice, the new government kept the Armed Forces small and under tight control by both President George Washington and Congress. In the fall of 1789, the President sought—and Congress, after sharp debate, granted—authorization for a force of militia to fight Indians in the Northwest Territory. When that expedition failed miserably, Congress in 1791 authorized a new regiment of Regular Army soldiers to resume the fight. A year later, after an even worse military disaster, Congress accepted Washington's plea for an additional five regiments but launched its first-ever oversight investigation—into the failed military operation—and forced a change in leadership of the expanded force.[14]

Where Congress fell short, however, was in legislation governing the use of militia. While authorizing the President to call up militia into Federal service, lawmakers refused to set standards for training or equipment. Nor did they provide funds to make the units more effective. No measures of standardization or modernization were enacted until the early 20th century.[15]

The disputes in the Washington and Adams administrations showed both the Presidents and the Congress to be assertive of their respective powers and yet deferential to the other branch. While they disagreed on some specific policies, they recognized their shared authorities on military affairs.

CONSTITUTIONAL RESPONSIBILITIES

Congress has two explicit and important responsibilities and one implicit but unquestionable responsibility with regard to war. Explicit in article I, section 8, of the Constitution are the powers "to declare war" and "to raise and support Armies," as well as the power to make rules organizing and governing the Armed Forces.[16] Implicit in its broad lawmaking power and the President's obligation to provide information on the state of the union is the power to conduct oversight of the executive branch. In addition, Congress may influence military strategy either directly, by legislating war aims, or indirectly, by creating certain military capabilities and offering recommendations. Finally, Congress has a role in conflict termination either through legislative enactments or Senate consideration of peace treaties.

What follows is not intended to be a legal analysis of Congress' proper role in wartime, but rather a legal/institutional/political history of how the legislative branch has acted during major conflicts. The constitutional responsibilities provide a useful framework for organizing and discussing the historical precedents.

CHAPTER 2

DECLARATION OF WAR

Congress has formally declared war in only 5 conflicts, but it has authorized the President to use the Armed Forces 15 other times, albeit with quite varied language and specificity. Sometimes the legislature has prodded the President to enter hostilities, while other times the President took the initiative, often in response to sudden developments. On at least one occasion, in 1815, the legislators refused to adopt the President's request for a declaration of war against Algeria. In some of the conflicts, Congress amended the President's proposed language in ways that limited how the executive could conduct the war. In short, Congress used its war power selectively and discriminatingly (see table 2–1).

There are many reasons why war has been declared so infrequently. Prior to World War II, the United States, like many other powerful countries, conducted limited military operations—shows of force, reprisal raids, protection of nationals, or quasi-economic interventions—that were not seen as rising to the level of war against another nation. Also, Congress usually met for only a few months a year, making it impractical to convene it for all but the most urgent matters of state.

Since World War II, there have been no authorizations of force using the "declare war" terminology because of a congressional concern about triggering the plethora of laws that apply only in wartime, particularly those that give the President broad powers over the economy and over the daily lives of citizens.[1]

A point of interest is that all American declarations of war, except in 1812 and 1898, blamed the other nation for initiating hostilities. The United States has always sought to portray its warlike actions as defensive, even when, as most historians judge the record with regard to Mexico in 1846, the United States committed an overt, provocative act.

EXPLICIT DECLARATIONS OF WAR

The new Nation's first formal declaration of war came in 1812 against Great Britain. President James Madison asked Congress for a declaration of war on June 1. The House of Represen-

Table 2–1. Congressional Actions Influencing Declarations of War	
Action	**Year**
Declined to declare war against Algiers, but did authorize use of force	1815
Added immediate $10 million appropriation to declaration of war with Mexico	1846
Initially pressed for Cuban independence with ultimatum to Spain and authorization of force; later agreed to request for declaration of war	1898
Promptly approved Korean aid and U.S. defense appropriations	1950
Authorized force in advance to pressure President Kennedy to remove any threat to the United States from Cuba	1962
Passed War Powers Resolution establishing procedures for involvement in hostilities	1973
Limited U.S. participation in peacekeeping force in Lebanon to assisting Lebanese forces; forbade engagement in combat except in self-defense	1983
Insisted on vote authorizing force in Gulf War, then adopted broad language	1991
Withheld veto override votes on law requiring end to Bosnian arms embargo, thereby adding pressure for Dayton talks	1995
Rejected White House language after September 11 attacks authorizing force to deter and preempt any future act of terrorism; limited authorization to those involved in attacks	2001

tatives passed its version on June 4 by a vote of 72–49, while the Senate debated the issue for several days. An amendment dropping the declaration of war and substituting language authorizing the President "to cause reprisals to be made on the public and private ships" of Great Britain failed on a tie vote. The Senate then approved the House language by a vote of 19–13 on June 17, and the measure was signed into law the next day. In language that would be closely followed on most subsequent occasions, the measure declared "that war be and the same is declared to exist between the United Kingdom . . . and the United States of America . . . and that the President of the United States is hereby authorized to use the whole land and naval force of the United States to carry the same into effect."[2]

The second explicit declaration of war came in 1846, when President James Polk, citing a border clash between Mexican and American troops, requested a vote for war on May 11. In the House, the administration added a preamble declaring "by the act of the Republic of Mexico, a state of war exists between that Government and the United States" to a bill providing funds for General Zachary Taylor's forces in Texas. After only 2 hours of debate, the House passed the bill by a 174–14 vote. The Senate followed the next day, after several failed amendments, with an overwhelming vote of 40–2. The final language declared a purpose—"enabling the government of the United States to prosecute said war to a speedy and successful termination"—before saying that "the President be, and he is hereby, authorized to employ the militia, naval, and military forces of the United States, and to call for and accept the services" of up to 50,000 volunteers. The bill went on to appropriate $10 million for the war and to provide rules for the organization and payment of the volunteer forces, including a 40-cent per day allowance "for the use and risk of their horses."[3]

In 1898, Congress passed two measures to force American intervention in Cuba. The first, on April 20, declared that "the people on the island of Cuba are and of right ought to be free and independent," and demanded that "Spain at once relinquish its authority . . . and withdraw its land and naval forces from Cuba and Cuban waters." The measure went on to say that the President "be, and he hereby is, directed and empowered to use the entire land and naval forces of the United States, and to call into the actual service of the United States the militia of the several States to such extent as may be necessary to carry these resolutions into effect." When Spain rejected an ultimatum to grant Cuban independence, President McKinley then asked Congress for a second law declaring "that war has existed since the twenty-first day of April" and repeating the "directed and empowered" language. That joint resolution passed promptly by voice votes in both chambers.[4] The first measure had been highly contentious and was subjected to several amendments as both Democrats and Republicans fought to be seen as the leading advocates of Cuban independence.

In April 1917, Congress heeded President Woodrow Wilson's request for a declaration of war against Germany, which had recently announced the resumption of unrestricted submarine warfare against U.S. and enemy shipping. The Senate voted 82–6 and the House 373–50 for the measure, which declared that

> the state of war . . . which has been thrust upon the United States is hereby formally declared; and that the President be, and he is hereby, authorized and directed to employ the entire naval and military forces of the United States and the resources of the Government to carry on war against the Imperial German Government; and to bring the conflict to a successful termination all of the resources of the country are hereby pledged by the Congress.[5]

Congress voted an additional declaration of war against Austria-Hungary the following December.

It is noteworthy that before the initial declaration of war, a Senate filibuster in the final days of the 64th Congress had blocked passage of the Armed Ship Bill sought by President Wilson. Besides authorizing U.S. merchant ships to arm and defend themselves, the bill would also have empowered the President to provide the weapons and ammunition for the ships and "to employ such other instrumentalities and methods as he may in his judgment and discretion deem necessary and adequate to protect such vessels and the citizens of the United States in their lawful and peaceful pursuits on the high seas." Some of the filibustering Senators opposed the bill because they feared that this last clause might be seen as authorizing an undeclared naval war.[6] Public outcry over the filibuster led the new Senate, sworn in only days earlier, to adopt the first rule in its history allowing debate to be ended by a two-thirds vote.

Following the Japanese attacks on Pearl Harbor and the Philippines, Congress quickly passed a declaration of war on December 8, 1941, by votes of 82–0 in the Senate and 388–1 in the House. Three days later, Congress passed similar language for war against Germany and Italy, and in June 1942, it passed war declarations against Bulgaria, Hungary, and Romania. All used the same language used in 1917, declaring a war "which has been thrust upon the United States" and authorizing and directing the President to employ all military forces and the Government's resources "to bring the conflict to a successful termination."[7]

EXPLICIT AUTHORIZATIONS OF FORCE

On many more occasions, Congress has adopted language authorizing the use of force against adversaries, but without the word *war* in the authorization. These measures also tended to be more lengthy and explanatory of the U.S. positions.

In 1797, President John Adams sought congressional support for a military buildup to counter French seizures of U.S. merchant ships. Congress was not supportive—until, in the spring of 1798, it became outraged over the publication of the XYZ dispatches reporting that the French had demanded bribes as a precondition to any discussions. Bipartisan majorities then rushed to pass various measures to strengthen American Armed Forces, as well as a law authorizing the President "to instruct and direct the commanders of [U.S.] armed vessels . . . to seize, take, and bring into any port . . . any such armed vessel which shall have committed or which shall be found hovering on the coasts of the United States, for the purpose of committing depredations on [U.S.] vessels."[8]

Adams considered asking for a formal declaration of war but remained hopeful of a diplomatic settlement and decided in favor of the military buildup. Several leading Federalists in Congress favored a declaration of war but lost votes on amendments for greater belligerency, such as seizing unarmed French merchant ships. On July 7, 1798, Adams signed into law legislation declaring "that the United States are of right freed and exonerated from the stipulations of the treaties" with France.[9] Two days later, he approved a more detailed law setting out provisions for handling captured vessels and specifically naming its target: "the President . . . is authorized to instruct [U.S.] commanders . . . to subdue, seize, and take any armed French vessel, which shall be found . . . on the high seas."[10] The so-called Quasi-War with France saw several successful U.S. naval engagements with French ships and ended with a diplomatic deal, the Convention of Môrtefontaine, in 1800.

In the spring of 1801, the bashaw of Tripoli declared war on the United States. With Congress out of session, President Thomas Jefferson consulted his Cabinet and decided to respond by sending a small squadron of four U.S. ships with strictly defensive orders. When Congress convened in December, Jefferson reported the developments and sought authorization for more aggressive action. The legislature passed an "Act for the Protection of Commerce and Seamen of the United States, against the Tripolitan cruisers" early in 1802. In the "whereas" clause, Congress said that Tripoli had "commenced a predatory warfare against the United States." The law went on to say: "it shall be lawful for the President" to instruct U.S. commanders "to subdue, seize and make prize" of ships and goods of Tripoli. More broadly, it declared that "it shall be lawful fully to equip, officer, man, and employ such of the armed vessels of the United States as may be judged requisite by the President . . . for protecting effectually the commerce and seamen thereof on the Atlantic Ocean, the Mediterranean and adjoining seas." The measure also declared as lawful "all such other acts of precaution or hostility as the state of war will justify, and may, in his opinion, require."[11] In 1804, Congress voted an extra 2.5 percent ad valorem duty on imports into the United States to pay for what the law called "carrying on warlike operations against the regency of Tripoli, or any other of the Barbary powers, which may commit hostilities against the United States."[12]

The United States signed a treaty with Tripoli in 1805, but trouble arose with Algeria a decade later. President James Madison specifically asked Congress to declare "the existence of a state of war" and provide "for a vigorous prosecution of it to a successful conclusion."[13] Congress responded with language identical to the 1802 law for Tripoli—charging predatory warfare in the "whereas" clause and declaring lawful "acts of precaution or hostility as the state of war will justify," but without formally declaring war.[14]

The American Civil War also involved authorizing legislation by Congress. President Abraham Lincoln took immediate action after the fall of Fort Sumter, including a call for 75,000 volunteer soldiers and a summons for Congress to convene in July 1861. Congress, which has the power to "provide for calling forth the Militia to execute the Laws of the Union, suppress Insurrections and repel Invasions,"[15] quickly passed legislation providing for the suppression of rebellion and authorizing the use of volunteers. The new law also gave the President the authority to determine when to use force to enforce the laws and suppress rebellion.[16]

Following the Vietnam War and the passage, over President Richard Nixon's veto, of the War Powers Resolution,[17] Congress repeatedly tried to embarrass, cajole, or force later Presidents into following the provisions of that law by seeking formal approval of Congress for troop deployments into hostile situations. The only occasion when a President acquiesced was in September 1983, when President Ronald Reagan agreed to a measure negotiated with Congress that explicitly invoked the resolution and authorized U.S. forces to continue to participate for 18 months in a United Nations–sponsored multinational force designed to police the promised settlement among Lebanese forces. The U.S. troops were restricted by a prior agreement with the government of Lebanon to providing "appropriate assistance to the Lebanese Armed Forces . . . and to further restoration of the sovereignty" of the Lebanese government over Beirut. That agreement also specified that "the American forces will not engage in combat" but could exercise self-defense. The law authorizing the use of troops cited that agreement and reiterated the right of the troops to take "protective measures."[18] This may be counted as an explicit authorization of force because U.S. deaths had been occurring despite the peacekeeping mandate, and defensive force was clearly mandated.

Congress also asserted that its 2001 authorization for force after the 9/11 attacks was given under the authority of the War Powers Resolution. While that authorization was passed primarily to wage war against the Taliban government of Afghanistan and the al Qaeda terrorists based in that country, the language was much broader. It authorized the President "to use all necessary and appropriate force against those nations, organizations, or persons he determines planned, authorized, committed, or aided the terrorist attacks that occurred on September 11, 2001, or harbored such organizations or persons."[19] Congress refused to accept a White House proposal for language also authorizing force "to deter and pre-empt any future acts of terrorism or aggression against the United States," but it did include prevention of future acts of terrorism by those connected to the 9/11 attacks as a reason for the bill.[20]

IMPLICIT AUTHORIZATION OF FORCE

In addition to the above measures explicitly authorizing the use of force, Congress has passed laws with less precise wording that nevertheless conveyed the intent to permit military action.

On April 20, 1914, President Woodrow Wilson addressed a joint session of Congress to ask for approval to use armed force to obtain the "fullest recognition of the rights and dignity of the United States" from Mexico. The triggering incident ostensibly was the temporary detention of some U.S. sailors in Tampico, but Wilson confided the real reason to congressional leaders: to prevent a German ship carrying weapons for the rebel government in Mexico City from landing. Within 24 hours, Congress overwhelmingly approved a joint resolution declaring "that the President is justified in the employment of the armed forces of the United States to enforce his demand for unequivocal amends for affronts and indignities against the United States." U.S. forces landed at Veracruz on April 23, where they encountered local resistance and suffered 19 deaths; they withdrew at the end of November.[21]

In September 1962, with concern growing about potential threats from Cuba, Congress adopted a joint resolution declaring that "the United States is determined—[a] To prevent by whatever means may be necessary, including the use of arms, the Marxist-

Leninist regime in Cuba from extending by force or threat of force its aggressive or subversive activities to any part of this hemisphere;—[b] To prevent in Cuba the creation or use of an externally supported military capability endangering the security of the United States."[22] A few weeks later, after Congress had adjourned, the Kennedy administration discovered evidence of nuclear-armed Soviet missiles in Cuba and was prepared to bomb and invade if an initial naval blockade did not secure removal of the missiles. President Kennedy did not believe legislation was needed to justify his actions. The resolution is an example of Congress's willingness to assert its authority to ensure a muscular response to emerging threats.

In August 1964, outraged by reports of attacks on U.S. Navy ships in the Gulf of Tonkin, Congress voted broad language in the knowledge that their resolution was, as State Department officials later argued, the functional equivalent of a declaration of war. The Tonkin Gulf resolution cited the Southeast Asia Collective Defense Treaty, which had created the Southeast Asia Treaty Organization (SEATO), and said, "the United States is, therefore, prepared, as the President determines, to take all necessary steps, including the use of armed force, to assist any [SEATO] member or protocol state . . . requesting assistance in defense of freedom." Regarding the attack on American ships, the joint resolution said, "Congress approves and supports the determination of the President, as Commander in Chief, to take all necessary measures to repel any armed attack against the forces of the United States and to prevent further aggression."[23] The language had been prepared in advance by the administration and, after brief debate, was passed overwhelmingly, 88–2 in the Senate and 414–0 in the House. In May 1965, Congress passed a $700 million emergency supplemental appropriations bill specifically for Vietnam operations. The overwhelming vote—only seven nay votes in the House, only three in the Senate—further confirmed legislative support for the ongoing war.[24]

CONTINGENT AUTHORIZATION OF FORCE

On occasion, Congress has voted to authorize force if certain conditions were met. This can be seen as backing and strengthening diplomacy with the threat of force. In terms of war powers, however, it surrenders the final decision on war to the President, who alone can judge whether the conditions have been met.

In 1858, Congress passed such a measure to support the President in diplomatic negotiations with Paraguay. The language declared "that for the purpose of adjusting the differences between the United States and the Republic of Paraguay . . . [the President] be, and is hereby, authorized to adopt such measures and use such force as, in his judgment, may be necessary and advisable, in the event of a refusal of just satisfaction by the government of Paraguay."[25] As things turned out, force was not necessary.

In the 1950s, similar contingent measures were used in Asia and the Middle East to deter hostile actions by American adversaries. President Dwight Eisenhower accepted Congress' necessary involvement in possible hostilities and welcomed actions that aligned the legislative branch with his diplomacy.

In response to Chinese Communist attacks on offshore islands under the control of the Nationalist Chinese (Kuomintang) government on Formosa (Taiwan), with which the United States had a mutual defense treaty, President Eisenhower asked Congress for a law committing the United States to the use of force. An important factor in both branches' willingness to adopt this legislation was the memory of 1949–1950, when senior U.S. officials openly declared Korea outside the American "defense perimeter," a stance that may have emboldened the North Koreans to attack South Korea. Soon after the start of the 84th Congress, with Democrats again in the majority, Eisenhower was able to sign a bill authorizing "the President to employ the Armed Forces of the United States for protecting the security of Formosa, the Pescadores and related positions and territories of that area."[26] The President was authorized to use force "as he deems necessary for the specific purpose of securing and protecting Formosa" and related territories. The House passed the joint resolution, 410–3, and the Senate, after rejecting restrictive amendments, did the same, 85–3.

A year later, to deal with instability in the Middle East, Eisenhower again asked Congress for blanket authority to oppose hostile threats to the nations of that area. The proposal, modified after extensive consultations with Members of Congress, drew on the precedent of the Formosa resolution and followed the

President's promise of the year before that "I will never be guilty of any kind of action that can be interpreted as war until the Congress, which has the constitutional authority, says so."[27] The measure combined anticommunism with an authorization to spend money for military and economic foreign aid to the area of the Middle East, thereby piggybacking a politically unpopular program on a muscular promise of American support for resistance to communist threats. The key language declared the preservation of the independence and integrity of the nations of the Middle East as a vital national interest and that "[t]o this end, if the President determines the necessity thereof, the United States is prepared to use armed forces to assist any such nation or group of such nations requesting assistance against armed aggression from any country controlled by international communism." The joint resolution contained a proviso that use of troops had to be "consonant" with the Constitution, so Members could argue that the President had to return to Congress before resorting to war.[28] The measure passed the House 350–60, and the Senate 72–19. But when President Eisenhower sent nearly 15,000 U.S. troops to Lebanon in July 1958 in what turned out to be a peaceful and uncontested operation, he did not seek further congressional action, although he consulted with Members.

In the view of many Members of Congress, the 1991 joint resolution authorizing U.S. participation in the first Gulf War was also contingent. The George H.W. Bush administration argued that an expression of congressional support for action against Iraq was welcome but not legally necessary. Some Senators opposed to immediate military action forced consideration of authorizing legislation, which ultimately passed by close margins, 250–183 in the House and 52–47 in the Senate. With a January 15 deadline for Iraqi compliance with United Nations Security Council (UNSC) resolutions looming, legislators acknowledged that their votes were the functional equivalent of a declaration of war.

The final language invoked the War Powers Resolution and authorized the use of force pursuant to 12 UNSC resolutions and then added the contingency: "Before exercising [this] authority . . . the President shall make available . . . his determination that—(1) the United States has used all appropriate diplomatic and other peaceful means to obtain compliance by Iraq with the United Nations Security Council resolution cited . . . and (2) that those efforts have not been and would not be successful in obtaining such compliance."[29] Last-minute talks failed, so the Presidential determination was easy to make, and coalition airstrikes began on January 17. In a futile attempt to force another vote on the war, the House on January 12 passed a concurrent resolution—which would not go to the President for his signature and thus would not have the force of law—expressing the sense that Congress must approve any offensive military action against Iraq. The vote in favor was large—302–131—but the Senate never took up the measure.[30]

The 2002 joint resolution authorizing force against Iraq was similarly contingent. It contained a requirement that the President determine that "reliance by the United States on further diplomatic or other peaceful means alone either (A) will not adequately protect the national security of the United States against the continuing threat posed by Iraq, or (B) is not likely to lead to enforcement of all relevant United Nations Security Council resolutions regarding Iraq."[31] The operative language was broad: "The President is authorized to use the armed forces of the United States as he determines to be necessary and appropriate in order to—(1) defend the national security of the United States against the continuing threat posed by Iraq; and (2) enforce all relevant United Nations Security Council resolutions regarding Iraq." All amendments to restrict the language were soundly defeated, and President George W. Bush ordered attacks on March 19, 2003.

CONFLICTS WITHOUT FORMAL AUTHORIZATION OF FORCE

Several major military operations—and about 200 minor ones—have been conducted without specific and controlling legislative action. In some cases, Congress saw no need to act; in others, Members were unsuccessful in getting formal legislation through both chambers and to the President. It is interesting and useful to consider these failed or incomplete attempts to authorize the use of force to appreciate how Congress views such action in a political context and not simply a constitutional or institutional one.

The United States inadvertently got involved in a guerrilla

war in the Philippines, which had been acquired from Spain in the 1898 war that Congress had authorized to secure Cuban independence. Congress was soon divided over whether and on what basis to continue U.S. control of the Philippines. Big Navy imperialists, most notably Theodore Roosevelt, saw the islands as a strategic asset important to becoming a Pacific power. Anti-imperialists wanted to avoid the costs, problems, and moral perils of empire. Because most U.S. political leaders opposed granting the territory statehood (many on racial grounds), the thorny issue of the Philippines' legal status troubled lawmakers. Meanwhile, the Filipino insurgents, who had been fighting Spain for independence and at first had been pleased with the American victory, entered into guerrilla warfare against the occupying forces that lasted from 1899 until 1902 and involved 126,000 U.S. troops, more than 4,000 of whom died in the course of over 2,800 engagements.[32]

By approving the Treaty of Paris on February 7, 1899, the U.S. Senate consented to American acquisition of the Philippines and, thereby, assumed the obligation to maintain law and order. In effect, Congress authorized the war in the Philippines in March 1899, by passing a bill maintaining the Regular Army at 65,000—compared to its early 1898 strength of 28,000—and allowing the enlistment of up to 35,000 volunteers for 28 months.[33] The Army stayed large after 1898—at least triple its prewar size—in part because of manpower requirements to deal with the insurgency in the Philippines. The conflict ended in 1902 with the capture of the guerrilla leader and the passage of the law establishing U.S. colonial administration.

In 1916, in response to a raid on Columbus, New Mexico, by forces under the control of Mexican rebel leader Pancho Villa, President Wilson sent General John Pershing and about 12,000 troops on a "punitive expedition." The Senate, without objection, approved a concurrent resolution—not intended to go to the President or become law—declaring "that the use of the armed forces of the United States for the sole purpose of apprehending and punishing the lawless band of armed men who . . . committed outrages on American soil and fled to Mexico is hereby approved." The House did not act on the Senate measure. In June, the President also mobilized 100,000 members of the National Guard for possible service, but they were never deployed outside the United States. Although Pershing never caught Villa, U.S. relations with Mexico improved, and U.S. troops were withdrawn in January 1917.[34]

The biggest war that Congress never authorized, or even tried to authorize, was the 3-year-long conflict in Korea, in which over 36,000 Americans died. Even a half-century later, the reasons for congressional acquiescence are still hard to fathom. What we know is that Harry Truman, despite spending 10 years in the Senate before becoming President and having cordial relations with the Democratic majorities in both chambers, embraced a strong and assertive view of Presidential power, particularly in national security matters. He was also surrounded by advisers with similar views of executive authority.[35]

When North Korean troops attacked South Korea on June 25, 1950, Truman, seeing a profound challenge to the international system created in 1945, promptly called for a UNSC session to deal with the crisis. Within 27 hours of the initial attacks, the Security Council—free from a Soviet veto because the Soviet delegate was boycotting the UN on another issue—passed a resolution urging North Korean withdrawal, declaring that a breach of the peace had occurred and calling upon member states to "render every assistance." This was the legal trigger for international use of force.

Truman believed that the North Korean attacks were Soviet-inspired, and he was more concerned about other Soviet-led attacks, particularly in Western Europe, than about the Korean Peninsula itself. At his first meeting with congressional leaders on June 27, Truman announced that he was ordering U.S. naval and air forces to give cover and support to South Korean troops. No one present asked about congressional action. All seemed pleased that the American help was in support of the United Nations. On June 30, when Truman had just approved General Douglas MacArthur's recommendation to commit U.S. ground troops, he met with 15 members. The Senate Minority Leader, Republican Kenneth Wherry of Nebraska, repeatedly pressed the President to consult with Congress before taking large-scale action. Truman defended his actions thus far but said he would go to Congress if there was a need for congressional action.

On July 3, he met with his advisers and the Senate Majority Leader, Democrat Scott Lucas of Illinois, who questioned the need for a congressional resolution. The advisers were also concerned that Republicans might raise the issue of Formosa, since Truman had rejected MacArthur's recommendation that the Chinese Nationalists be brought into the fight. The administration had drafted a measure for congressional leaders to introduce that dealt only with Korea and commended the United Nations—deliberately not mentioning Truman—for aiding South Korea and expressed "the sense of Congress that the United States continue to take all appropriate action with reference to the Korean situation to restore and maintain international peace and security in support of the Charter of the United Nations and of the resolutions of the Security Council of the United Nations."[36] Truman ultimately decided not to call Congress back from its Fourth of July recess, and the message he sent on July 19 called not for authorization for combat but rather for $10 billion in emergency spending to fight the war. Congress proceeded to pass these and related measures, showing its support of the war.

In short, it seems that both the President and the Democrats in Congress thought that formal congressional authorization of combat in Korea was not legally or politically necessary and that legislation might ignite a controversy over Formosa and undercut the rationale that the United States was only helping the United Nations. Republican criticism of Truman's action did not gain wider support until the Chinese Communists intervened in massive numbers and the war stalemated.

In 1965, President Lyndon Johnson sent 23,000 troops into the Dominican Republic, ostensibly to protect American lives and property but mainly to prevent pro-communist elements from taking power. Johnson consulted with some Members of Congress regarding his action but did not seek or receive formal legislative blessing. The only congressional action was a House resolution approved in September that, without naming any countries, endorsed the unilateral use of force to prevent communist takeovers in the Western Hemisphere. U.S. forces were withdrawn in September 1966.[37]

When pro-communist elements overthrew the government of Grenada in October 1983, President Ronald Reagan sent 7,300

U.S. military personnel to rescue U.S. citizens, mostly medical students, and to establish a more friendly government. The operation lasted only a few days. The Democratic-controlled House voted to invoke the War Powers Resolution for the action, but the Republican-controlled Senate failed to agree.

In December 1989, President George H.W. Bush sent 13,000 U.S. military personnel to overthrow the government of Panama, headed by Manuel Noriega, and to protect the lives of U.S. citizens. The President sent a notice of action called "consistent" with the War Powers Resolution. Congress was out of session when the troops were sent, and the fighting was over by the time it convened on January 23, 1990. Before adjourning, the Senate had passed an amendment supporting diplomatic, economic, and military options "to restore constitutional government to Panama and to remove General Noriega," but it had also defeated an amendment specifically authorizing the President to use military force to secure Noriega's removal. On February 7, the House passed a resolution saying that the President had acted "decisively and appropriately in ordering U.S. forces to intervene in Panama."[38] The same day, the legislators approved $42 million in emergency aid to the new Panamanian government, thus further demonstrating their support for the military action. The invasion force was withdrawn in mid-February 1990.

Much more controversial was the U.S. intervention in Somalia in 1992–1994. As that African nation disintegrated into warring clans, Congress adopted several measures urging humanitarian relief. As conditions became acute during the final weeks of his administration, President George H.W. Bush decided to send 25,000 U.S. troops to assure the delivery of relief supplies. When the new Congress convened and President Bill Clinton was inaugurated in January 1993, the Senate quickly passed by voice vote a joint resolution authorizing the President to use U.S. force pursuant to the UNSC resolution calling for "a secure environment for humanitarian relief operations." House action did not come until May 25, when that chamber amended the Senate measure to set a 1-year time limit on the troops before adopting it, 243–179. Since the language differences were never resolved, the President never received an agreed bill to sign into law.[39]

After the United Nations took control of the operation in May 1993, U.S. troop levels dropped to about 4,000, most of which were offshore as a ready reaction force. When UN and U.S. forces suffered casualties in late summer, the House and Senate adopted amendments to the defense authorization bill calling for consultations and reports from the administration. Before those amendments were reconciled, 18 U.S. Army Rangers were killed in a failed raid to capture a hostile clan leader. After consulting with lawmakers determined to force an end to U.S. involvement in Somalia, the President announced that he planned to withdraw U.S. troops by March 31, 1994. Congress promptly adopted amendments to the defense appropriations bill prohibiting funds for U.S. military operations in Somalia after that date.[40]

In 1994, Congress was generally hostile to the Clinton administration's growing determination to intervene in Haiti to restore the democratically elected government of Jean-Bertrand Aristide, but nothing with teeth was ever enacted into law. U.S. ships began enforcing a UN embargo on Haiti in October 1993, and Congress shortly thereafter passed amendments that ultimately were signed into law as part of the defense appropriations bill. The key language stated "the sense of Congress" that funds should not be spent for U.S. military operations in Haiti unless those operations were authorized in advance by Congress, necessary to protect or evacuate U.S. citizens, or vital to U.S. security and urgent before Congress could act.[41]

After the Security Council voted on July 31, 1994, to authorize "all necessary means to facilitate the departure from Haiti of the military leadership," President Clinton sent additional warships into the area and recalled some Reservists. The Senate voted unanimously its sense that the UNSC resolution did not constitute authorization for the deployment of U.S. forces, but that amendment was rejected in conference. On September 19, U.S. troops began arriving in what turned out to be an unopposed intervention because of the last-minute agreement by Haitian military leaders to leave office and the country. In early October, Congress passed a joint resolution saying that the President should have sought congressional approval before sending troops, supporting a prompt and orderly withdrawal, and requiring monthly reports. UN forces took over responsibility for Haiti on March 31, 1995.[42]

Congressional efforts to guide policy on the Balkans were more influential but not definitive. President Clinton and many Members of Congress from both parties were critical of Serbian military activities and were eager to end the UN arms embargo with respect to Bosnia. The President favored multilateral lifting of the embargo, while Congress pressed for unilateral action. At the same time, legislators adopted several amendments expressing the sense of Congress that U.S. ground combat troops should not be sent to the Balkans and that prior approval of a deployment would be necessary. In July 1995, veto-proof majorities passed a bill requiring an end to the arms embargo but permitting successive 30-day waivers to allow the withdrawal of a UN peacekeeping contingent. The bill also specifically declared that it could not be construed as authorization for any deployment of U.S. forces into Bosnia. Clinton vetoed the bill on August 11 but simultaneously authorized U.S. participation in North Atlantic Treaty Organization (NATO) airstrikes against Serb positions and launched a diplomatic offensive that culminated in the Dayton peace agreement on November 21. Congress never voted to override the veto.[43]

Efforts to forbid or restrict the deployment of over 25,000 U.S. troops to help enforce the Dayton agreements were unsuccessful. Conferees were never appointed to reconcile the various measures voted in the few weeks before the settlement took effect on December 14.[44]

When President Clinton ordered NATO-approved airstrikes against Serbia in support of Albanians in Kosovo on March 24, 1999, Congress again took numerous votes on several proposals but failed to adopt in both houses any measure either authorizing or constraining the operation.[45]

U.S. forces were sent into several Caribbean countries during the first half of the 20th century, often for many years. Those operations were in Haiti (1915–1934), the Dominican Republic (1916–1924), and Nicaragua (1909–1910, 1912–1925, and 1926–1933). Because the initial interventions were usually to protect American lives or interests in unsettled conditions, no authorization by Congress was seen as necessary. Subsequent approval of military appropriations containing funds for the overseas operations was considered to be sufficient legislative consent. Over time, however, reports of problems or misconduct in various countries occasionally prompted congressional hearings, notably on the Philippines, Haiti, and the Dominican Republic.

As this summary of conflicts and associated congressional actions shows, the legislative branch has been careful and discriminating in its authorization of force (see table 2–2, next page). At times, it has adopted measures short of what the President has requested. Only sparingly has it formally declared war. More often, it has approved the use of force, sometimes contingent on subsequent events and Presidential determinations. On occasion, Congress has sought to guide or restrict the use of force to particular purposes set forth in the authorizing legislation. When lawmakers failed to enact specific legislation permitting the use of force, they subsequently demonstrated support for the military operation by approving funds and other laws for them.

Sometimes Congress has pressed belligerency on a reluctant chief executive—notably in 1812, 1898, and 1962. At other times, the President maneuvered so that Congress became willing to authorize warfare—notably in 1798, 1846, 1955, 1957, and, arguably, 2002. On many other occasions, both branches of government agreed, without much debate or dissent, that the national interest required a militant response.

CONFLICT AVOIDANCE

Congress has tried at different times to prevent U.S. involvement by enacting both substantive prohibitions and procedural hurdles. In the 1930s, spurred by revisionist analyses that blamed "merchants of death" for World War I, Congress passed a series of neutrality acts. The first, in 1935, prohibited the export of "arms, ammunition, or implements of war," barred U.S. ships from carrying arms to belligerents, and restricted travel by American citizens on ships of belligerent countries.[46]

When that law was set to expire in 1936, Congress extended it for another year and added language prohibiting Americans from making loans or extending credit to belligerents. In 1937,

Table 2–2. Authorizations of Force		
Declarations of War	**Explicit Authorization of Force**	**Implicit Authorization of Force**
Britain, 1812	Quasi-War, 1798	Spain, 1898
Mexico, 1846	Tripoli, 1802	Mexico, 1914
Spain, 1898	Algeria, 1815	Cuba, 1962
Germany and Austria-Hungary, 1917	Civil War, 1861	Vietnam, 1964
Japan, Germany, Bulgaria, Hungary, and Romania, 1941–1942	Lebanon, 1983	
	9/11 attackers, 2001	

the legislators passed an act specifically forbidding the export of arms, ammunition, and implements of war to Spain, which did not fall under the existing law because it was torn by a civil war. In May 1937, Congress voted for a third neutrality act, imposing a rigid embargo on countries at war and those experiencing civil strife. The revised law added a prohibition on the arming of U.S. merchant vessels.[47]

Congress softened the law after Germany invaded Poland but still made it unlawful for U.S. vessels to carry passengers or any articles to belligerent states, for American citizens or ships to go to or through combat zones, and for American citizens to travel on ships of belligerents. The law also banned the arming of U.S. merchant vessels. When lawmakers learned of plans to send newly built torpedo boats to Britain, the Naval Affairs Committees pushed through legislation banning the disposal of any equipment unless the Service chief certified that "such material is not essential to the defense of the United States." President Roosevelt then pressured the Chief of Naval Operations to grant that certification for 50 destroyers he wanted to send to Britain in return for various basing rights.[48] Congress finally repealed most of the neutrality laws less than a month before Pearl Harbor.

Table 2–2. Authorizations of Force (continued)		
Contingent Authorization	**Conflicts without Formal Authorization**	**Conflict Avoidance Measures**
Paraguay, 1858	Philippines, 1899–1902	Neutrality Acts, 1935–1939
Formosa, 1955	Mexico, 1916	Ban on sending draftees outside of Western Hemisphere, 1940–1941
Middle East, 1956	Korea, 1950–1953	Restriction on transferring U.S. military equipment, 1940
Gulf War, 1991	Dominican Republic, 1965	Ban on sending U.S. ground troops into Laos or Thailand, 1969
Iraq, 2002	Grenada, 1983	War Powers Resolution, 1973
	Panama, 1989	Hughes-Ryan Amendment restricting covert operations, 1974
	Somalia, 1992–1994	Arms Export Control Act, 1976
	Haiti, 1994	Ban on aid to or activities in Angola, 1976
	Bosnia, 1995	Ban on U.S. military operations in Nicaragua, 1986
	Kosovo, 1999	Personnel ceilings in Colombia, 2000

Another prewar restriction, enacted as part of the peacetime draft law in 1940 and again in 1941, barred the sending of draftees outside the Western Hemisphere. This provision was quickly repealed after the declaration of war against Japan. When the draft was renewed in 1948, the law required that draftees receive at least 12 weeks of training in the United States before they could be sent overseas.[49]

In response to the conduct of the Vietnam War and disclosures about secret agreements and covert operations, Congress tried to limit the President's foreign policy powers that could lead to war. The War Powers Resolution of 1973 established procedural requirements and reports when U.S. forces were sent into hostile situations. The National Commitments Resolution expressed the view that only affirmative action by Congress can create a commitment to use force. The Case Act required congressional notification of all executive agreements. The Arms Export Control Act gave Congress notification of and a veto over foreign arms sales. The Hughes-Ryan Amendment required Presidential approval and prompt notification to Congress of covert operations by the Intelligence Community.

The most far-reaching of these measures was the War Powers Resolution, enacted over President Nixon's veto in 1973. It requires the President to consult with Congress before introducing U.S. Armed Forces into hostile situations and during their deployment. It requires a report to Congress within 48 hours in most circumstances when U.S. forces equipped for combat are sent abroad. The law also requires termination of the U.S. operation within 60 days, unless Congress has authorized the use of force or declared war. It also says that Congress can force the removal of U.S. forces from hostilities by passage of a concurrent resolution— a measure that is not subject to Presidential veto. This last provision became constitutionally suspect after the 1983 Supreme Court decision in *INS v. Chadha*, which ruled a legislative veto in immigration law unconstitutional.[50]

Substantive prohibitions on the deployment of American military personnel were also enacted. In December 1969, Congress passed an amendment forbidding the introduction of U.S. ground combat troops into Laos or Thailand. In 1976, Congress passed three different measures forbidding military assistance to forces in Angola or spending for "any activities in Angola other than intelligence gathering." In the 1980s, Congress passed several measures intended to block assistance to the Nicaraguan opposition force, widely known as the Contras. In 1986, Congress passed a law specifically barring U.S. military personnel from operating in Nicaragua. In recent years, Congress has written into law ceilings for U.S. military personnel and civilian contractors in Colombia.[51] These preventive or precautionary measures were in addition to laws terminating U.S. military involvement in Southeast Asia, Somalia, and Rwanda.

In addition to these statutory provisions, lawmakers made many failed attempts to enact binding legislation either supporting or opposing major conflicts. Perhaps Members believed—or hoped—that "sense of Congress" amendments would actually compel Presidents to follow the requirements of the War Powers Resolution or other laws and seek advance approval for major military operations. Perhaps savvy legislative leaders protected their party's man in the White House by deft parliamentary maneuvers to avoid political embarrassments. Perhaps domestic political considerations or their own reading of the Constitution stopped some lawmakers from challenging the Commander in Chief. Perhaps Members wanted to cast votes and yet avoid real responsibility for their recommended policies. Whatever the explanation, the recent record is muddled, and its precedents are poor guides to action. By failing to complete legislative action, lawmakers left their intentions unclear and their claimed powers unused.[52] Where Congress did complete action, however, it has on occasion forced the executive branch to alter its preferred policy or to act somewhat differently.

CHAPTER 3

RAISE AND SUPPORT ARMIES/ MAKE RULES GOVERNING CONDUCT

After authorizing the use of force, Congress has usually also exercised its power to "raise and support Armies" and "make rules for the government and regulation of the land and naval forces." The exercise of these indisputable legislative powers can constrain the Commander in Chief's actions and shape the use of force (see table 3–1).

MANPOWER

The Revolutionary generation in America was profoundly distrustful of standing armies. The framers of the Constitution included several provisions to guard against an armed force that could threaten domestic liberty, such as the prohibition on any funds for the Army lasting beyond 2 years. John Adams preferred a strong Navy to deal with foreign threats and only reluctantly accepted the Army that Congress thrust upon him. Thomas Jefferson willingly slashed the Army by 40 percent and agreed to the founding of West Point only because it was to be an engineering school. American leaders, until the advent of airpower, generally viewed the Army as a last-ditch defense against an unlikely invasion and as a frontier police force protecting settlers against Indians. Most Americans believed that if wars were to be fought on U.S. soil, state-run militias could and would do the job.

To support major military operations, therefore, Congress had to provide authority, funds, and incentives for additional military personnel. In 1798, but only after disclosure of the

XYZ correspondence, Congress rushed to pass 20 different bills strengthening national defense. The measures included a quadrupling of the Army, a ten-fold increase in the Navy, creation of a separate Navy department, the reestablishment of the Marine Corps, and a 10,000-man provisional army that could be raised for 3 years at the President's discretion. To help recruit that army, Congress

Table 3–1. Congressional Actions Influencing the Raising and Supporting of Forces	
Action	**Year**
Repeatedly refused to strengthen and standardize militia despite preferring reliance on it	1790–1914
Created Mediterranean Fund with special tax to pay for new ships and operations against Barbary pirates	1804
House of Representatives rejected new warships before war but increased Army	1812
Rejected requests for conscription	1813–1814
Added 50,000 volunteers with same pay and benefits as regulars for war with Mexico; later added 160-acre land benefit for those completing one year of service or suffering death or disability	1846
Denied requests by President Polk for larger Regular Army and establishment of lieutenant general position	1846
Blocked $2 million contingency fund requested for peace settlement by filibustering Wilmot Proviso	1847
Increased force from 400,000 requested by President Lincoln to 500,000 at start of Civil War	1861
Voted additional 500,000 men day after Bull Run defeat	1861
Voted first retirement pension for officers with 40 years of service	1861
Added funds for "submarine inventions" and ways to make ships invulnerable	1862, 1864
Voted $50 million in unrestricted funds and two extra artillery regiments 7 weeks before declaration of war against Spain	1898

offered a bounty of $10 for a 3-year enlistment and provided that enlisted men would be free from personal arrest for debt or contract during their service.[1] The bounty may not seem like much unless one realizes that privates were paid only $3 per month. A few months later, to increase the Army by a dozen more regiments, Congress increased the bounty to $12 and monthly pay to $5 and

Table 3–1. Congressional Actions Influencing the Raising and Supporting of Forces *(continued)*	
Action	**Year**
Increased President McKinley's request for Navy by tripling number of battleships, doubling number of torpedo boats, and almost tripling number of destroyers	1898
Cut proposed increase in Regular Army and voted larger volunteer force	1898
Pressured for coastal defense, resulting in splitting of fleet	1898
Filibustered bill to arm merchant ships prior to declaration of war against Germany	1917
Forced President Wilson to accept law granting broad reorganization authority	1918
Impeded aid to countries threatened by Nazi Germany through passage of Neutrality Acts; gradual revisions allowed more help	1930s
Restricted transfer of U.S. military equipment, almost blocking destroyer-for-bases deal with Britain	1940
Voted peacetime draft with President Roosevelt's silent support	1940
Pressed President Roosevelt to keep George Marshall as Army Chief of Staff	1943
Rejected call by President Johnson for draft lottery Elevated status and protected budget of Special Operations Forces	1967 1986
Raised taxes/tariffs to pay bulk of costs of Quasi-War, Barbary conflict, Mexican-American War, Spanish-American War, World War II, Korean conflict	1794– 1950s
Depended on borrowing for War of 1812, Civil War, World War I, Vietnam War, Iraq war	1812– present

guaranteed daily rations of "one pound and a quarter of beef, or three-quarters of a pound of pork, eighteen ounces of bread or flour, a gill [four ounces] of rum, brandy or whiskey."[2]

In the months before the War of 1812 was declared, Congress took the lead in enacting preparedness measures because the executive branch failed to provide detailed recommendations. As one scholar concluded, "In truth, the secretary of war was made a clerk to the congressional committee." While the Madison administration favored a 10,000-man increase in the Regular Army, Congress approved a 13-regiment (25,000-man) increase for a 5-year enlistment. The law included a $16 bounty and a promise, upon honorable discharge, of 3 months' pay and 160 acres of land. If soldiers died while in service, their heirs would get the land. Widows of officers who died in service were also promised half pay for 5 years. A few months later, the lawmakers voted an additional 15,000-man increase in the Army, providing a bounty of $16 for an 18-month enlistment and guaranteeing the same pay, clothing, rations, and "provisions for wounds or disabilities" as other soldiers—except for the land. When these benefits still proved inadequate, Congress eventually raised the bounty to $40 and allowed the transfer of state militia units directly into the Army. It rejected, however, repeated calls by the Secretary of War to institute a draft. Lawmakers also failed to make recommended changes in the militia system.[3]

To supplement General Zachary Taylor's Regular Army forces in Mexico in 1846, Congress voted to allow the President to recruit up to 50,000 volunteers for at least 12 months. They were promised the same pay, allowances, and death or disability benefits as Regular Army soldiers. In January 1847, Congress added an enlistment bounty of $12 and extended the term of service to 5 years. Only a month later, to raise an additional 10 regiments, Congress voted to give a warrant for 160 acres of land—or $100 in interest-paying Treasury scrip—to anyone who was disabled in service or was honorably discharged after at least 12 months of service, or to the heirs of a soldier killed in action. Three weeks later, as the 29th Congress was about to expire, lawmakers voted to add a reenlistment bounty of $12.[4]

In the Civil War, Congress retroactively approved Lincoln's call for 75,000 volunteers and then increased his request for an additional 400,000 men for 3 years to 500,000. After the Union defeat at Bull Run, Congress voted another 500,000 men for the duration of the war. Lawmakers included a $100 bonus for death, disability benefit, or honorable discharge.[5] Subsequent laws added various administrative provisions, including a $25 enlistment bounty, creation of units of former slaves, and freedom for slaves and their families who served the Union. When these measures proved inadequate, Congress enacted the first draft law, discussed below.

In 1898, Congress voted for two additional artillery regiments and $50 million in unrestricted funds for national defense soon after the explosion that sank the battleship USS *Maine* in Havana harbor, 7 weeks before war was declared. Once war began, Congress voted additional legislation. One provision increased the pay for enlisted personnel by 20 percent for the duration of the war.[6] President William McKinley used his authority to raise volunteers by summoning initially 125,000 men and then an additional 75,000. The recruiting goals were largely met by the time the war ended 4 months later, but problems in transporting and provisioning the units prompted a highly critical investigation in the aftermath.

CONSCRIPTION

Despite manpower shortages during the War of 1812 and repeated requests from the Secretary of War to enact some form of conscription, Congress strongly resisted the idea, preferring to rely upon volunteerism and state militias. In the Civil War, however, the manpower needs proved too great. Congress voted a draft law for "all able-bodied male citizens" aged 20 to 45 in March 1863. It required up to 3 years of service and allowed few exemptions, which were judged by three-man enrollment boards in each congressional district. The boards were appointed by the President and had to include a practicing physician. Men could legally avoid the draft by hiring a substitute or paying a commutation fee of $300. Penalty for resisting the draft was a fine of $500 or imprisonment for 2 years. After much criticism and deadly draft riots in New York and elsewhere, Congress repealed the commutation fee a year later and set the penalty for forcible resistance at $5,000 or 5 years in prison. It added, however, a provision allowing conscientious objectors to be assigned to hospital service. While the draft itself accounted for only 6 percent of the men who served in the Union Army, and only 46,347 of those drafted did not hire a substitute or pay the commutation fee, it helped to stimulate voluntary enlistments.[7]

To raise the army for World War I, Congress also had to enact a draft. This time, lawmakers permitted deferments for essential work in agriculture or industry but did not allow substitutes or commutation. They also let local boards of civilian volunteers decide individual cases. Nearly three-quarters of those who served in the wartime army were draftees. Enactment was delayed for 6 weeks by disputes over the minimum age (eventually set at 21) and whether Theodore Roosevelt would be allowed to raise and lead a 100,000-man corps of volunteers, a proposal that the administration ultimately rejected.[8]

In 1940, despite strong isolationist sentiment in Congress and the country at large, lawmakers enacted the first peacetime draft. President Franklin Roosevelt was reluctant to endorse the legislation until his 1940 election opponent supported the measure and public opinion soared to 71 percent in favor, but he let Army Chief of Staff General George Marshall work with pro-interventionist groups to guide the legislation through Congress. The President was active in recommending huge increases in defense spending, which Congress and the public were willing to support as conditions worsened in Europe with the fall of France to the German army. The draft bill as enacted in September required only 12 months of service and provided that the troops could not be used outside the Western Hemisphere. In the summer of 1941, when the draft had to be extended to avoid the wholesale discharge of barely trained troops, Roosevelt again let Marshall take the lead. The Senate approved a 1-year extension by 45–30, and the House passed the measure thanks to a single vote and fast gaveling by Speaker Sam Rayburn. Immediately after Pearl Harbor, Congress repealed the Western Hemisphere restriction on the deployment of draftees and extended the term of service for the duration of the war. Deferments went for hardship cases and men in war industries and agriculture. The system of local draft boards was retained. The draft brought over 10 million men into uniform during the war. Volunteers accounted for another 6 million men and women. The draft expired in 1947 as the Armed Forces were being substantially demobilized.[9]

As Cold War tensions increased in 1948—with such dramatic events as the pro-communist coup in Czechoslovakia and the Soviet blockade of Berlin, which prompted the allied airlift in response—Congress renewed the draft, which stayed on the books until 1973. Lawmakers accepted the need for a large, standing force as a Cold War requirement, and the draft was selective rather than universal, depending on monthly quotas. The law provided enough authority to raise the forces needed in Korea and Vietnam. It did require that draftees receive at least 12 weeks of training before being sent abroad.[10] In the early years, the legislative battles were over proposals to have universal military service. The draft was extended with little dispute in 1950, barely a month before the Korean War broke out, and again in 1951, 1955, 1959, and 1963.

In 1967, with the Vietnam War spurring demonstrations and anti-draft actions, Congress rejected President Lyndon Johnson's request for a draft lottery and instead called for expeditious prosecution of violators. President Richard Nixon used the draft for Vietnam needs but endorsed the idea of a volunteer army. Lengthy debate in 1971 culminated in a 2-year extension of draft authority, but under a new lottery system and with sharply reduced student deferments. The law also provided big pay increases for enlisted personnel to help stimulate volunteers and capped annual inductions at 140,000.[11] The Nixon administration gradually reduced its draft calls in advance of the 1972 elections and the January 1973 Paris Peace Accords, which ended U.S. combat in Vietnam.

OFFICER CORPS

On occasion, the Senate has used its advise and consent power to block military nominations or promotions. It is noteworthy, however, that only the President can dismiss military commanders. The impeachment power extends only to "civil officers" of the government.[12]

President John Adams tangled with Alexander Hamilton and his Federalist allies in Congress over the staffing of the Provisional Army. Hamilton insisted on allowing only Federalist officers and favored a Senate effort to create the new rank of full general for George Washington. Adams, fearing that Washington would overshadow his Presidency if such an honor was bestowed, launched a diplomatic effort that ended the Quasi-War with France a few months later.[13]

President Polk tried in 1846 to reestablish Washington's former rank of lieutenant general, so he could name his Democratic ally, Senator Thomas Hart Benton of Missouri, as commander over his Whig field commanders, Winfield Scott and Zachary Taylor. Congress refused to acquiesce.[14] In 1864, however, Congress rushed to reward Ulysses S. Grant with that prestigious rank. Members also made a point of giving President Lincoln lists of those they favored for appointment to major general, brigadier, and lesser ranks. Republicans in Congress criticized what they saw as the domination of the officer corps by declared Democrats. In fact, 80 of the 110 generals in the Union Army in 1861 were Democrats. By 1863, four-fifths of the brigadier generals and major generals were still said to be Democrats. One reason is that Lincoln had granted general officer commissions to Democratic politicians to broaden political support for the war.[15]

Aspiring politicians sought military service. In 1898, both Theodore Roosevelt and William Jennings Bryan commanded locally recruited volunteer regiments, but only Roosevelt actually got to see combat in Cuba. In World War I, enactment of a draft was delayed for several weeks by controversy over a proposal by Roosevelt to command his own corps of fighters for Europe.

In World War II, some of the sharpest civil-military disputes President Franklin Roosevelt had with his commanders came when he overrode their objections to give officer commissions to his son Elliot and to political friends. Several Senators intervened in the fall of 1943 to insist that General Marshall be kept as Army Chief of Staff rather than being given command of the forces being assembled to invade Europe. They considered him too valuable at home and his likely successor too weak in defending the Army's interests.[16]

During the Vietnam War, Senators on occasion blocked action on routine military nominations until they obtained information on military operations previously withheld from Congress. In the Iraq war, anticipated congressional opposition reportedly derailed a promotion for Lieutenant General Ricardo Sanchez, USA.

VETERANS' BENEFITS

Congress from the earliest days enacted various forms of veterans' benefits as part of inducements for voluntary enlistments. Revolutionary War officers were later promised half-pay for life, but few received full benefits. Congress did not enact a pension for needy veterans of all ranks until 1818 and not until 1832 a pension for all who had served at least 6 months—in a war that had ended nearly 50 years earlier.[17]

In subsequent wars, Congress front-loaded calls for volunteers with various benefits. In addition to death and disability payments, lawmakers were willing to grant warrants for land, a popular benefit. Following the Civil War, in response to large and well-organized veterans' organizations, Congress enacted a comprehensive system of military pensions, survivor benefits, and hiring preferences into Federal jobs for Union soldiers. In the South, Confederate veterans had to settle for state-funded pensions and soldiers homes.

Post-service benefits for officers were sporadic prior to the Civil War. Congress voted small severance pay disbursements at the time of force reductions in 1796, 1800, 1802, and 1815. With no pensions, many officers held on to their positions as long as possible. In 1860, for example, 19 of 33 Army officers at colonel or above were veterans of the War of 1812. The following year, Congress voted retirement benefits for men with 40 years of service—basic pay for their rank, plus allowance for four rations per day.[18]

In World War I, Congress tried to avoid the pension problem by enacting War Risk Insurance for soldiers to pay small premiums to obtain life insurance and future medical care. The program was poorly run and inadequately financed, so in 1921 Congress set up a comprehensive system of veterans' hospitals. Instead of a pension, veterans were promised a bonus to compensate for wages lost while in military service, to be paid in 1945. In 1932, veterans massed in Washington, DC, in the so-called Bonus Army and drove Congress to pay the bonus in 1936.

Events associated with the Bonus Army kept veterans' issues before Congress and the public so that even before the end of World War II, Congress enacted the G.I. Bill, which promised a free college education and medical care, temporary unemployment insurance, and guaranteed home purchase loans. Somewhat lesser benefits were enacted for veterans of the Korean and Vietnam wars.[19] Except for the enlistment bonuses and death and disability benefits, most of the generous programs for veterans have been enacted after war's end, sometimes in tribute for their service, sometimes out of guilt for their sacrifices.

EQUIPMENT AND SUPPLIES

In addition to raising manpower for major conflicts, Congress has the responsibility of equipping and supporting the troops in the field and the ships at sea. Whenever Congress votes to build facilities or award contracts, political and parochial concerns may come into play—as they have throughout American history.

When Congress in 1794 authorized construction of six frigates to respond to Barbary Coast threats, lawmakers were sharply divided, with coastal representatives overwhelmingly in favor and inland representatives largely opposed. The Washington administration wisely chose to build each ship at a different seaport, from Norfolk, Virginia, to Portsmouth, New Hampshire. Contracts for timber went to the Carolinas and Georgia. Cannons were ordered from Connecticut and Maryland firms, and related iron implements came from New Jersey and Pennsylvania firms.[20]

Four years later, Congress created a separate Navy Department, in part because the contracts for the frigates had been badly mismanaged. A congressional committee investigating the matter charged the War Department with "enormous expenses and unaccountable delays."[21]

Although the War of 1812 was provoked by disputes over maritime issues, neither Congress nor the Madison administration saw much need for a naval buildup. Most Republicans—in Congress and in Madison's cabinet—shared the view that navies were too costly. Three months before war was declared, the House rejected its committee's recommendation for 10 new frigates and approved only funds to return 3 mothballed ships, while allowing purchase of timber for 3 more, if they were later authorized. Madison himself switched from planning a land campaign only to favoring a war at sea, largely for practical reasons. Naval victories and Army defeats reinforced political support for the Navy as the war proceeded, and Congress even voted for four battleships and six heavy frigates in the winter of 1813.[22]

Prior to 1898, military appropriations were usually quite detailed, unlike the lump sum measures adopted for later conflicts. The Army appropriation funding the expansion just before the War of 1812 had such items as $2,500 for the purchase of books, maps, and instruments, and $150,000 for the purchase of horses. The Army appropriation in 1814 included $2,036,000 for clothing and $460,000 for camp and field equipage. The Navy appropriation the same year granted $120,000 for medicines and hospital stores and $71,788.10 for clothing for men in the Marine Corps.[23]

The same specificity was found in the funding for the war with Mexico. Among the line items in the Army appropriation for August 8, 1846,[24] were $50,000 for transporting officers' baggage when traveling on duty without troops, $40,000 for purchase of saltpeter and brimstone, and $30,000 for military and geographical surveys west of the Mississippi.

In the Civil War, Congress coupled the standard line items with additional broad discretionary authority. In response to reports of abuses, legislators tightened the laws on contracting, requiring all major contracts to be in writing and various reports to be filed. Lawmakers also pushed for the development of new weapons. An 1862 law authorized the Navy Secretary "to test plans and materials for rendering ships and floating batteries invulnerable." An 1864 law gave $25,000 for the testing of "submarine inventions."[25]

At the start of the Spanish-American War in 1898, Congress greatly increased President McKinley's recommendations for an enlarged Navy by approving three battleships instead of the one requested, as well as doubling the number of torpedo boats and almost tripling the number of destroyers.[26]

With war raging in Europe but America still at peace, Congress moved in 1916 to enact several measures of military preparedness. It voted an increase in the Regular Army and provided for the reorganization and equipping of the National Guard in the various states. Lawmakers also enacted a major shipbuilding program, accelerating a requested 5-year program (including the production of 10 battleships) into 3 years. To equip and supply the

Armed Forces, Congress created a Cabinet-level Council of National Defense and authorized the President to place orders for defense items and seize plants if necessary.[27]

As evidence of congressional willingness to be practical even while controlling the purse strings, Congress enacted legislation as early as 1799 allowing the Armed Forces to buy some basic items, such as clothing, medicines, and camp equipage, in advance of the annual appropriations. The authority was broadened in 1861 in what came to be known as the "feed and forage law," a form of which is still on the books.[28] By the 20th century, Congress was more willing to enact lump sum appropriations, or bills with only a few line items. This allowed military managers more discretion, including the ability to conceal secret programs (the most notable example was the Manhattan Project to build atomic bombs). Today, defense appropriation bills for half a trillion dollars are enacted using only about 53 broad line items, only 12 of which are under a billion dollars.[29]

In the 21st century, Congress financed the Afghanistan and Iraq wars almost entirely by emergency supplemental appropriations, measures that necessarily receive less thorough scrutiny and get no input from the Armed Services Committees, which specialize in military issues.

Congress has played only a limited role in determining grand strategy during major military operations. Yet in their actions prior to conflicts, lawmakers have made de facto strategic decisions by funding certain kinds of forces and associated weaponry. By choosing in 1792 to rely on state-run militias, without Federal requirements or material support, Congress limited the development of ground combat capabilities until the outbreak of the Civil War. By finally choosing to build a blue-water Navy in the 1790s, Congress enabled the United States to deal with the Barbary pirates and even to challenge the British Royal Navy. By refusing to embrace steam-powered, all-metal warships until late in the 19th century, both branches of government limited America's abilities to use sea power to defend or promote its economic and security interests. And by its enthusiasm for airpower in the 1920s and 1930s, Congress helped to advance that technology and build the core competencies for America to fight far more effectively and successfully in World War II. Similarly, in the 1980s, Congress forced a reluctant Pentagon to put significant resources into special operations forces, which then became important components of the wars of the 21st century.

WARTIME FINANCING

A necessary element in raising and supporting military forces is obtaining the resources to finance their development and operations. Until after the Civil War, the revenue and spending responsibilities were centered in the same committees—Ways and Means in the House, Finance in the Senate. In 1865, Congress assigned spending decisions to new Appropriations Committees, where they remain today.

The Revenue Committees took their jobs seriously and reported numerous measures over the years to finance the wars American entered. In 1798, Congress voted for its first direct tax on Americans—a levy of 50 cents for each slave and a graduated tax on houses, from 40 cents for one valued at $200 to 30 cents per $100 valuation for houses costing $500 or more. Lawmakers also voted to borrow up to $5 million for the military buildup.[30]

To finance the extra costs of the additional ships, men, and operations to deal with the Barbary powers, Congress voted in 1804 to assess a 2.5 percent ad valorem tax on top of import duties already in law, with the proceeds deposited in a special "Mediterranean Fund" to be used solely for Barbary-related expenses.[31]

The War of 1812 posed significant funding problems for the U.S. Government because restrictions on trade with Europe drastically cut the receipts of duties on imports, the primary source of revenue until the enactment of income taxes in the Civil War and again just before World War I. Congress enacted tax measures and doubled existing duties, but these steps failed to generate anticipated income; loans by issuing bonds financed 79 percent of the $87 million cost of the war.[32]

The $82 million spent on the war with Mexico was financed 41.8 percent by taxes and customs and 58.2 percent by borrowing. The costs were quite small in terms of the growing economy—only 3.6 percent of gross national product (GNP). The Civil War, by contrast, cost $2.3 billion, or nearly 75 percent of GNP. Nearly 91 percent of the Union's expenditures were financed by money creation and debt. The Federal Government resorted to the first national paper money, the "greenback," and the first income tax, a slightly progressive measure that charged 3 percent on incomes of $600 to $10,000 and 5 percent above $10,000. Banker Jay Cooke also led a surprisingly successful drive to sell government bonds widely among the population—a technique repeated with success during the two World Wars.[33]

The Spanish-American War of 1898 lasted only a few months, and the cost of $270 million was equivalent to only 1.8 percent of GNP. The conflict was easily financed, 66 percent by taxes and customs, 34 percent by money creation and debt.[34] Because the income tax had been ruled unconstitutional, thus preventing its use until ratification of the 16th Amendment in 1913, Congress resorted to excise taxes on such items as cosmetics, chewing gum, playing cards, and admission to theaters and other places of entertainment. Tobacco and beer taxes were doubled. Lawmakers also voted an excise tax on long distance telephone calls—quite a luxury at the time—that was not repealed until 2006.[35]

World War I proved to be an enormous economic challenge to the U.S. Government. The costs were huge—$32.7 billion, equal to 43 percent of one year's GNP—and the rapid military buildup imposed serious dislocations on economic activity. The draft drained men from shops and factories, and purchases of food and equipment drove up prices of basic commodities. Revenues covered only 24 percent of the immediate costs of the war, so Congress passed a stiff, highly progressive income tax and corporate "excess profits" tax that brought in almost 60 percent of wartime revenues.[36]

In addition to financing the costs of war, Congress sought to counter the inflationary effects with a law empowering the President to fix prices on products such as wheat and coal and stimulate production of necessary items. In response to an investigation of inefficiencies in defense contracting, Congress forced President Woodrow Wilson to accept a law giving him broad authority to reorganize the government as well but required that he appoint Bernard Baruch as the economic czar.[37]

World War II was an even greater challenge, costing over $360 billion, nearly double one year's GNP. Taxes accounted for 41 percent of the cost, with excess profits tax rates soaring to 95 percent and income tax exemptions dropping, so that the number of people paying rose from 7 million to 42 million in a highly progressive system. By 1945, nearly 90 percent of U.S. workers had to submit tax returns. Congress also gave President Roosevelt broad power to regulate the economy and impose wage and price controls and rationing of food, clothing, and consumer goods. However, it rejected his suggestion of a labor draft, thus sometimes leading to labor shortages in particular areas.[38]

The broadly based income tax has remained a major source of government revenues. The Korean War's $50 billion cost was financed entirely by revenue measures and without borrowing. Congress restored World War II–era tax rates and permitted widespread wage and price controls. Lawmakers also passed the Defense Production Act to expand Presidential powers over the economy.[39] Defense spending then stayed high throughout the Cold War.

During the Vietnam War, President Lyndon Johnson resorted to budgetary tricks to minimize the apparent costs of that conflict to avoid cuts to his Great Society domestic programs. After having passed a tax cut in 1964, Congress enacted temporary 10 percent tax surcharges on individual income and corporate taxes in 1968 and 1969. Later revenue bills had a net effect of cutting taxes. In an attempt to contain the inflationary impact of rising budget deficits and an expansionary monetary policy, the Nixon administration imposed price controls in phases from 1971 to 1974.[40]

The 1991 Gulf War proved to be low-cost for the United States because other nations contributed nearly 80 percent of the $61 billion outlay to help offset U.S. expenditures. The conflict also occurred at a time of monetary contraction and budget deficit reduction.[41]

The conflicts after the 9/11 attacks, including the Iraq war, have been financed by borrowing because of President George Bush's commitment to Federal tax cuts. Counting budget estimates through fiscal year 2008, those conflicts will have cost nearly $700 billion.[42]

In assessing this record, Congress probably deserves positive marks for its actions to pay for conflicts by substantial revenue increases in World War I, World War II, and Korea. Deft diplomacy also recovered the costs of the 1991 Gulf War. In contrast, Congress fell short in financing measures for the War of 1812 and combat operations in Vietnam and Iraq.

Since the start of the Korean War in 1950, the United States has maintained standing forces sufficient to handle all major military operations except Korea, Vietnam, and Iraq without a draft, significant force expansion, or extra taxes. Congress has shifted its "raise and support" efforts to long-term questions of force modernization, research and development for dramatic new technologies, and pay and benefits for the volunteer force. For both the executive and the legislative branches, readiness accounts have mainly been bill payers for other activities and occasions to score debating points rather than a high priority.

The historical record shows that Congress has been discriminating and influential in how it has chosen to raise and support military forces. In hindsight, some of its actions look unwise or unfortunate, while others appear prescient and helpful. In both cases, Congress believed it was acting within its rules and in accordance with its constitutional powers.

CHAPTER 4

STRATEGY

Congress can influence the conduct of major military operations in three ways: by the size and capabilities of the forces lawmakers raise and support, by explicit goals they set in approving the use of force, and by recommendations they may offer regarding the conduct of the war (see table 4–1). While the Commander in Chief obviously is constrained by the available military capabilities, there is much more debate on whether he should accept congressionally mandated goals.

In the Quasi-War with France, Congress approved the seizing only of armed warships, not French merchant ships. This helped dictate a more limited and defensive conflict, but John Adams was not particularly eager to conduct full-scale war in any case. Against the Barbary powers, Congress authorized broad powers not only to protect commerce and seamen, but also to take precautionary actions. Lawmakers did not seek to constrain Presidential strategy.

In the War of 1812, the administration changed its strategic plan twice, and Congress followed in support. Madison initially expected to fight a quick ground war in Canada to gain negotiating leverage. He then saw a need to protect U.S. merchant ships in the early months of a war, and so the conflict began as a maritime war only. Later, U.S. ground forces attempted to invade Canada but were thwarted by logistical problems and military defeats, thus forcing the United States to rely again on naval warfare, where the results were more promising, at least to public morale. Early in 1814, two Federalist Congressmen offered amendments trying to block any invasion of Canada, but they were voted down by large margins.[1]

By specifically authorizing the use of volunteers against Mexico in 1846, Congress permitted a ground offensive strategy into Mexico. But the war aims remained unsettled. There was broad agreement on securing Texas with a border on the Rio Grande and on acquiring California, but some Members favored the conquest of "all of Mexico." The conflict also got embroiled in the slavery issue when the House passed the Wilmot Proviso to forbid slavery in any newly acquired territories, and the Senate refused to pass war funding measures with such language.

The Civil War also found Congress divided on war aims and the treatment of slaves. In keeping with Lincoln's formulation, the initial legislation authorized troops only to suppress rebellion and enforce Federal laws. There soon arose tough questions over what to do with slaves who came under Union control. Congress pushed faster than the President for emancipation of slaves and creation of fighting units of former slaves. In July 1861, lawmakers voted for emancipation of slaves employed in arms or labor against the Union. In April 1862, Congress voted to abolish slavery in the District of Columbia. In July, it passed a bill defining rebels as traitors and ordering the confiscation of their property, which meant freeing their slaves. In 1864, Lincoln pocket-vetoed a radical

Table 4–1. Congressional Actions Influencing Strategy	
Action	**Year**
Voted to end slavery in the District of Columbia and to emancipate some slaves prior to decision by President Lincoln	1861–1862
Foreclosed annexation of Cuba by Teller Amendment	1898
Endorsed postwar international security organization	1944
Barred U.S. ground combat operations in Laos or Thailand	1969
Limited number of U.S. military personnel and civilian contractors in Colombia	2000–present

reconstruction law that Congress had passed in its final hours. Most Members of Congress who consulted with the President, the Secretary of War, and various generals had simple strategic advice: "attack, attack, attack," and "on to Richmond." They, like the President, were dissatisfied with General George McClellan's lengthy preparations for operations and with roundabout approaches toward the Confederate capital. They did not challenge General Ulysses Grant's attrition warfare and continued to raise and support armies to carry it forward.[2] The Joint Committee on the Conduct of the War (JCCW) pressured both Lincoln and the generals summoned to testify to be more aggressive militarily and more supportive of abolitionist war aims. Often, they uncovered factions within the Union armies more supportive of their goals and more willing to criticize their commanders.[3]

In the war with Spain in 1898, Congress specifically authorized only the goal of obtaining Cuban independence from Spain. The Teller Amendment denied any intent to turn the island into a U.S. possession. But lawmakers had not anticipated the question of the Philippines, and even the President hesitated before concluding that the islands should be kept under American control.

Since Woodrow Wilson was quite clear about his war aims—the Fourteen Points—even before entering World War I in 1917, Congress implicitly endorsed them by voting broad authority for the President to act. As the German military and government collapsed in 1918, some Republican legislators called for "unconditional surrender," but Wilson ignored them. Only by its subsequent action in rejecting the Versailles Treaty did Congress seem to reject some of the President's key war aims.

In World War II, as well, Congress left strategy up to the President. This turned out to be quite fortunate, since public opinion in the wake of Pearl Harbor favored a Japan-first strategy rather than Franklin Roosevelt's Germany-first plan. There were several debates on the Europe-first approach, and one Member of Congress even introduced resolutions, never acted on, calling for a postponement of the invasion of Europe in order to concentrate on the Pacific war. Nor did Congress question the strategic bombing campaign up to and including the atomic bomb attacks on Japan. President Roosevelt avoided debate on war aims by proclaiming the goal of "unconditional surrender" early in 1943. When one Senator asked General George Marshall what the overall military objectives of the Joint Chiefs were, "Marshall declined to answer on the ground that they were so secret he could not tell 'anybody' outside of a few of his own staff members."[4]

Neither the Truman administration nor Congress gave serious strategic thought to war aims in Korea at a point when it might have made a difference. At first, U.S. leaders seemed content to restore the status quo ante bellum—a division of the peninsula along the 38th parallel. But flush with success after the Inchon landings, they embraced the chance to unify Korea as a pro-Western democracy.[5] When Chinese Communist forces intervened to prevent that outcome, Truman and his advisers rejected General MacArthur's call for attacks inside China. The strategic debate over what to do about sanctuary areas continued through the public debate and congressional hearings following MacArthur's firing and recurred later during the Vietnam War.

Congress granted the President broad discretionary authority in the Formosa Resolution of 1955 and the 1956 Middle East Resolution and specifically endorsed preventive action in Cuba in 1962. The Tonkin Gulf Resolution also empowered the President to "prevent further aggression" in Southeast Asia. The biggest strategic debates during the Vietnam War were over the use of airpower against North Vietnam and ground combat forces in border sanctuary areas. The Senate and House Armed Services Committees used hearings and speeches to press for fewer restraints on targets selected in the north. But after the 1970 invasion of Cambodia, Members angrily debated and eventually passed legislation to require the withdrawal of U.S. forces from that country. Earlier, Congress had enacted a prohibition on the use of ground combat forces in Laos or Thailand, a restriction that limited U.S. strategic options.

In Lebanon in 1983, Congress specifically limited the U.S. peacekeeping force to a defensive strategy of backstopping the Lebanese army and protecting itself.

Congress has also foreclosed large-scale operations in Latin America by voting low ceilings for U.S. military personnel in specific countries. Under pressure from Congress, the Reagan administration voluntarily limited the number of U.S. military personnel posted to El Salvador at 55. Congress later wrote into law ceilings on U.S. military personnel and civilian contractors in Colombia.[6]

While Congress imposed no strategic constraints in authorizing force against Iraq in 1991 and 2002, it did refuse to accept administration-proposed language after the 9/11 attacks that would have authorized preventive force against any and all terrorists. The law as enacted allowed only attacks against those somehow involved in the 9/11 attacks. When President Bush subsequently announced that he would follow a policy of preventive war against terrorists, Congress held debates but took no legislative action.

In short, Congress generally has been reluctant to take formal action that might be seen as restricting military strategy. Because there have been exceptions, there are precedents for such restrictions in special circumstances. Most notably, Congress can set war aims—both positive goals to be achieved and self-denial restrictions—as was done by the Wilmot Proviso and the Teller Amendment.

On the other hand, because grand strategy involves the use of all the instruments of national power, it is evident that Congress has been quite assertive in nonmilitary matters. At the height of World War II, it passed resolutions endorsing an international security organization, which became the United Nations. In 1948, the Senate passed another resolution supporting the creation of a U.S. military alliance to defend Europe. The congressional initiative creating the Iraq Study Group in 2006 was another attempt to fashion an alternative strategy for the Iraq war.

In these various ways, Congress has acted to set or at least influence the strategy followed in major conflicts. The paucity of examples underscores the general acceptance by lawmakers that the President has the lead role in crafting grand strategy as well as operational tactics.

CHAPTER 5

OVERSIGHT

The first special investigating committee established by Congress probed a military operation, the 1792 expedition against Indians in the Northwest Territory under the command of General Arthur St. Clair that ended with over half the U.S. force killed or wounded. For the next century, about half of all investigations conducted by Congress were related to the activities of the Armed Forces (see table 5–1).[1] Many of these congressional inquiries occurred during major military operations of longer duration, while others took place retrospectively. Some resulted in remedial legislation; virtually all ended with reports, speeches, and news articles. In the second half of the 20th century, about 10 percent of all congressional hearings were on defense and foreign policy.[2]

Congress has long asserted an implicit authority to inquire into the execution of its laws. In the Legislative Reorganization Act of 1946, it particularly mandated standing committees "to exercise continuous watchfulness" over programs and agencies under their jurisdiction. Most common historically are what some scholars call "fire alarm" hearings, investigating reported problems or scandals. With large, standing Armed Forces and a much expanded government, congressional committees have increased their frequency of "police patrol" hearings in what might be called prospective oversight.[3]

While formal committee hearings have been the most common venue for legislative oversight, Members of Congress have also met frequently with the President and senior leaders to discuss or be briefed on military and foreign policy matters. Ever since Members of the Continental Congress made frequent visits to General Washington's headquarters, legislators have wanted to visit war zones and get firsthand information about the ongoing conflict.

As noted in the discussion of strategy, Congress rarely has been directly involved in advocating specific military courses of action. But the very act of inquiry—through the subjects probed and the frequency and intensity of questioning—can amount to indirect strategic recommendations. The hostile 1967 Senate Armed Services Committee investigation into bombing strategy over North Vietnam, for example, prompted the Johnson administration to expand its target lists just before the hearings began so that the

Table 5–1. Congressional Actions Influencing Oversight	
Action	**Year**
Established special committees during Barbary conflict, War of 1812, Civil War, Philippines conflict, World War II, Korean War	1804–1950s
Conducted oversight by standing committees during Korean War, Vietnam War, and conflicts since 1980	1950s–present
Demanded detailed reports in Quasi-War, War of 1812, Mexican-American War, Civil War, Vietnam War, Gulf War, post–9/11 Afghanistan, Iraq war	1798–present
Ordered military supply contracts to be in writing	1862
Pressed Lincoln to replace McClellan and other generals perceived as unsuccessful	1861–1864
Conducted investigations that exposed atrocities in Philippines campaign	1902
Held hearings that defused public outrage over firing of General Douglas MacArthur	1951
Held hearings on air war restrictions over North Vietnam that prompted increase in number of allowed targets	1967
Passed Hughes-Ryan amendment barring Central Intelligence Agency covert operations unless President approves and Congress is notified	1974

administration could report a policy more likely to meet committee approval.[4]

In the early years of the Republic, congressional investigations of military operations usually involved letters or resolutions of inquiry that led to executive branch reports, which then were made public, often with comments and suggestions by Members. During the Quasi-War with France, Congress investigated cost overruns and delays in shipbuilding, raised inquiries, and got reports on shipbuilding, coastal fortifications, munitions manufacture, manpower needs, and the effectiveness of the trade embargo.[5]

The conflict with the Barbary powers led to one special committee that probed the conduct of an overland operation to determine whether to pay special compensation to the Tripolitan leader's brother, who had allied with the American forces. Other committees were established to consider the many reports of naval engagements and other developments provided by the executive branch.

In 1809, the House authorized a special committee to investigate Army spending irregularities after a debate in which some Members challenged the principle of such investigations. The majority agreed, however, with such stirring comments as those of former three-term Speaker of the House, Nathaniel Macon (D–NC), who said, "If we cannot inquire into the state of the Army, it follows that the Army belongs to the President and not to the nation," and Timothy Pitkin (Federalist–CT), who commented, "I know that it has been said that we have no right to inquire into the conduct of the Commander in Chief of the Army of the United States. I have reflected on this subject considerably, and have made up my mind, that this House, as the grand inquest of the nation, has a right to make this inquiry."[6]

In the months leading up to War of 1812, there were numerous inquiries and reports between the executive and the legislature. The practice continued after the declaration of war. In July 1813, a Vermont Congressman proposed the creation of a special committee "to inquire into the causes which have led to the multiplied failures of the arms of the United States on our Western and Northwestern frontier." The measure was postponed until December and then modified to request a report from the President, after which it was approved 137–13. Throughout the war, the Madison administration was forthcoming in supplying reports. Barely a month after the burning of the capital, for example, the President submitted a detailed 75-page report on the disaster.[7]

During the war with Mexico, Congress created a committee to investigate the conduct of the war, but only, as it turned out, a few weeks before it learned of the signing of the peace treaty. Otherwise, it relied on resolutions of inquiry seeking documents from the President.[8]

Most far-reaching of all wartime oversight committees was the Joint Committee on the Conduct of the War, established during the Civil War. It began with proposals to investigate two early Union defeats but was broadened to cover all aspects of the conduct of the war. Other committees investigated matters under their particular jurisdiction, such as a House investigation of fraud and mismanagement in government contracting, but the JCCW was the most active and the most comprehensive. It met almost daily when Congress was in session but kept its deliberations secret until issuing reports. Members of the committee traveled widely both to battlefields and to northern cities to pursue its investigations. It held 272 formal sessions, issued 11 reports, and had 8 meetings with the President and many more with the Secretary of War.[9]

The JCCW served as a source of both criticism and constructive advice. Besides investigating various Union defeats, it also exposed Confederate atrocities against Union soldiers, uncovered defects in the manufacture of naval equipment, and condemned the slaughter of defenseless Indians by the Colorado state militia. The committee was not impartial, however. As one leading historian concluded, the committee "showed a preference for the generals who endorsed forward movement and frontal assaults and who spoke of vigorous action; it expressed disdain for generals who emphasized planning, logistics, strategy, and a hands-off policy toward southern civilians."[10]

While historians at this distance can take a more benign view of the committee's influence, it is a fact that two later Presidents, Woodrow Wilson and Harry Truman, were so troubled by its reputation that they worked assiduously to prevent the reestablishment of anything like the JCCW during either of the World Wars.

The war with Spain in 1898 ended with an armistice in just under 4 months, perhaps too quickly to prompt Congress to set up any special committees. To preempt such investigations, President William McKinley appointed a special group, the Dodge Commission, to conduct an after-action review while Congress was in recess. That commission held hearings and exposed numerous shortfalls in military contracting, provisioning, and logistics that set the stage for major Army reforms over the next several years.[11]

Oversight of the 4-year conflict in the Philippines produced damaging testimony of U.S. atrocities. A special Senate Committee on the Philippines, chaired by Henry Cabot Lodge (R–MA), was forced by anti-imperialists to hold several weeks of hearings in 1902. Under sharp questioning, military and civilian officials acknowledged use of the "water cure" to interrogate prisoners and indiscriminate burning of civilian housing, resulting in punishment of at least 44 U.S. soldiers for cruelties against Filipinos.[12]

Just 3 days after the declaration of war against Germany in 1917, the Senate began considering a proposal for a new JCCW. An amendment creating such a committee was approved 53–31 as a rider to the food control bill. President Wilson fought fiercely (and successfully) to have the provision dropped in conference. As a result, the primary vehicle for oversight was the Senate Military Affairs Committee, under the chairmanship of a Democrat hostile to Wilson, George Chamberlain of Oregon. His committee held numerous hearings, and he made a speech in January 1918 sharply criticizing the management of the war and declaring, "The military establishment of the United States has fallen down." Chamberlain's proposal for a war cabinet independent of the President was not adopted, but Congress did pass the Overman Act, which gave extraordinary powers to reorganize the government for greater efficiency and effectiveness.[13]

During World War II, one scholar calculated, "Congress conducted more than a hundred investigations . . . exploring many aspects of war policy but falling short of investigating the actual conduct of the war." Missouri Senator Harry Truman chaired the committee that did the most extensive oversight of military matters, the Special Committee to Investigate the National Defense Program. It deliberately focused on contracting issues relating to industrial mobilization rather than military operations or strategy. Other active committees were the House equivalent to Truman's panel, the Tolan Committee, the Senate and House Small Business Committees, and the Military Affairs Committees.[14] By early 1943, General Marshall complained that "upwards of thirty committees have concerned themselves with duplicated and overlapping inquiry into War Department activities since January 1943 resulting in tremendous loss of time and diversion from our military responsibilities."[15] Despite this complaint, Marshall frequently met with Members of Congress during the war.

While some militarily sensitive information was withheld from Congress, the four defense committees developed good working relations with the executive branch. The committees got regular reports on the progress of the war and conducted some investigations on production and procurement issues. President Franklin Roosevelt had off-the-record meetings with lawmakers to discuss the Casablanca Conference and gave public reports to Congress on other major wartime conferences. Some Senators also visited the war zones and reported back in secret sessions. Only five senior appropriators in each body were told of the Manhattan Project to develop atomic weapons. They shepherded the money bills through the Congress, with the secret project funds included in lump-sum measures. At one point, the House Members, concerned about delays in the program, refused to approve additional funds. They relented after being taken to the Oak Ridge, Tennessee, facility.[16]

Congress also took legislative action looking toward postwar problems. Secretary of State Cordell Hull consulted frequently with Members of Congress. In return, they insisted that the United Nations Relief and Rehabilitation Administration[17] be established by legislation through both houses rather than by executive agreement, which would not have been subject to congressional review or approval. Both chambers passed resolutions endorsing the idea of a postwar international peace and security organization, and Members were delegates to the conference that drafted the United Nations Charter.[18]

In response to President Truman's firing of General Douglas MacArthur in April 1951, the Senate conducted a wide-ranging, 7-week investigation into the strategy and conduct of military operations for the Korean War. The Armed Services Committees in both chambers had summoned U.S. military leaders to hearings soon after the conflict broke out and continued that practice throughout the war. The Senate Armed Services Committee held 14 hearings on Korea in the summer and fall of 1950, 8 more in 1951, and another 6 in 1952—all in addition to the 41 days of joint hearings with the Foreign Relations Committee related to the MacArthur controversy. Two additional days of hearings were held in May 1952 to investigate riots at a UN-run camp for prisoners of war that had resulted in 30 casualties, an admission of mistreatment by the U.S. commander, and the replacement of the camp leadership.[19]

During the Vietnam War, the number of hearings was even greater. The Armed Services Committees tended to hear from and reflect the views of military officers who preferred fewer civilian restraints on operations, in particular a more aggressive bombing campaign against Hanoi. In 1966, the Senate committee developed a conservative critique of the administration strategy, following it in 1967 with several days of hearings specifically on the bombing strategy and target lists. The Foreign Relations Committee, by contrast, was the center of criticism of the war. Early in 1966, Chairman J.W. Fulbright (D–AR) held 6 days of televised hearings, mostly of opponents of the war. Relations between Fulbright and the Johnson administration became so strained that Secretary of State Dean Rusk refused to appear in any more public hearings of the committee on the subject of the war.[20]

After Richard Nixon became President, the Foreign Relations Committee was even more active in building the case against the war, and Congress became more active in considering restrictive legislation. The Senate Armed Services Committee, by contrast, explored controversies related to what might best be called military integrity: the firing of Air Force General John Lavelle for unauthorized airstrikes over North Vietnam, the secret bombing of Cambodia in 1969–1970, and the military spy ring that obtained secret materials from Henry Kissinger for the Joint Chiefs of Staff.[21]

In most other major military operations in recent decades, the President met with congressional leaders just prior to making a speech to the Nation regarding his actions, and there usually were classified briefings open to all Members of Congress. The Military, Foreign Policy, and Intelligence Committees had their own briefings, but there were few hearings that tried to suggest alternative strategies during the various conflicts or systematically assess "lessons learned" from the operations. A notable exception occurred in the early 1980s, when the Armed Services Committees drew on the flaws in such missions as the 1980 attempt to rescue Americans held hostage in Iran to fashion the Goldwater-Nichols Defense Reorganization Bill of 1986.[22]

Congress commissioned a major Pentagon study of the 1991 Gulf War but spent its time before and after the conflict mainly considering how to downsize the force and the defense budget as the Cold War was ending.

Perhaps the low point in legislative-executive relations over a post–Cold War military operation came in October 1993, when the Clinton administration was forced to reassess its policy in Somalia after the deaths of 18 U.S. soldiers in a failed attempt to capture a hostile clan leader. The beleaguered Secretary of Defense, Les Aspin, went with Secretary of State Warren Christopher to consult with Members in a special meeting held on the floor of the House of Representatives. Aspin said, "I'm up here to get your ideas about what we should do." The lawmakers, angry about the policy and unaccustomed to having their ideas sought in advance of actual decisions, turned the meeting into a disaster for Aspin and his colleagues.[23]

The Clinton administration kept Congress at a distance during its later military interventions abroad. Republican control of Congress after the 1994 elections created a powerful adversarial relationship on both domestic and foreign policy matters. While the President submitted the standard war powers notifications when military forces were sent into action, most of the operations were so short in duration that Congress did not conduct special oversight. The most extensive prior consultations with legislative leaders occurred before the August 1998 strikes on terrorist camps in retaliation for U.S. Embassy bombings in Kenya and Tanzania and before the March 1999 airstrikes against Serbia in defense of Kosovo.[24]

After the 9/11 attacks, the Defense and Foreign Policy Committees held hearings and briefings on administration actions in Afghanistan and, later, Iraq. Since both operations were initially successful, congressional oversight focused mainly on such symbolic issues as the adequacy of armored vehicles and body armor for troops. The Senate Armed Services Committee also conducted 9 days of hearings into the detainment of prisoners at Guantanamo Bay and the abuse of prisoners in Iraq. Its House counterpart held only 2 days of hearings on Abu Ghraib because the chairman said he was reluctant to summon commanders from the war zone.[25] As security conditions in Iraq deteriorated, congressional committees continued to hold hearings but did not seek to recommend alternative military strategies. Various Members and committees commissioned reports on a variety of Iraq and Afghanistan issues, especially by the Government Accountability Office. The Iraq Study Group of 2006 was created by Congress with the aim of crafting a bipartisan policy for Congress and the administration. The Democratic-controlled 110th Congress has increased its oversight of the war and has attempted to pass restrictive legislation.

While Presidents tend to resent and resist oversight that exposes problems, that investigative function is at the core of all other legislative activity—writing laws, approving budgets, and deciding how or whether to support major military operations. What is most pronounced in the historical record but has been sadly lacking in recent years is vigorous oversight of Presidents by Congresses controlled by their own partisans.

CHAPTER 6

TERMINATION

Congress has played a key role in the termination of conflicts. Since wars often end with treaties, Senate approval is necessary, and the Senate has a long history of amending and rejecting even the most significant international agreements (see table 6–1).

Although the military engagements of the Quasi-War with France ended early in 1800, a formal agreement was not signed until the end of September. When President Adams presented the Convention of Môrtefontaine to the Senate, that body at first rejected it by a 16–14 vote that fell short of the two-thirds majority required. As public support for the deal became evident, enough Members changed their votes to allow it to pass 10 days later by a 22–9 vote. The Senate insisted, however, on amending the convention by dropping one article and limiting its duration to 8 years. This required further negotiations with France and the agreement of Napoleon, which finally came only after Thomas Jefferson became President.[1]

The War of 1812 also ended with a treaty, one that mentioned none of the maritime issues that provoked the conflict and basically returned things to the status quo ante bellum. Nevertheless, the Senate approved it unanimously barely 24 hours after its submission.[2]

Termination of the war with Mexico was more complicated because the Treaty of Guadalupe Hidalgo had been negotiated contrary to Presidential instructions. President Polk nevertheless submitted the treaty for ratification, having concluded that the deal would be popular—as it proved to be, winning Senate approval 37–14.

The Civil War ended with the surrender of Confederate forces, but the process of reconstruction and the return of the southern states to regular status lasted until 1877. The 1898 war with Spain concluded with an armistice followed by a treaty. To improve the chances of approval, McKinley named three Senators to the five-man delegation sent to negotiate. The resulting treaty was ratified with only two votes to spare because of considerable opposition to its inclusion of U.S. control of the Philippines. News reports of an attack on U.S. troops by insurgents helped tip the balance in favor of the treaty at the last minute.[3] The Philippine insurgency ended with the capture of the rebel leader, Emilio Aguinaldo, and U.S. colonial rule was codified in the Organic Act of 1902.

Table 6–1. Congressional Actions Influencing War Termination	
Action	**Year**
Amended treaty ending Quasi-War, forced further negotiations	1801
Three senators named to delegation negotiating treaty with Spain	1898
Rejected Versailles Treaty that ended World War I	1919
Tie vote on resolution calling for withdrawal of U.S. forces intervening in Soviet Russia, prompting order for withdrawal within days	1919
Voted on resolution asking for immediate return of U.S. occupation troops from Germany, prompting withdrawal announcement within days	1923
Barred further military operations in Cambodia following U.S. withdrawal	1970
Forced U.S. air combat operations in Southeast Asia to end	1973
Rejected last-minute requests for aid for South Yemen	1975
Wrote into law Clinton administration promise to withdraw U.S. troops from Somalia	1993

Withdrawal of U.S. forces from the various Caribbean interventions of the early 20th century was usually accomplished by executive agreements and without legislation. After failing in a 1929 vote to cut off funds for U.S. Marines in Nicaragua, Congress succeeded in 1932 in blocking funds for U.S. troops to supervise Nicaraguan elections.[4] The troops came home the following year. In recent decades, U.S. interventions in the Dominican Republic, Haiti, and Panama ended by turning control over to UN forces or the local government—all without action by Congress.

World War I ended with an armistice on November 11, 1918, but the Senate rejected the Versailles Peace Treaty, which President Wilson had helped to negotiate. When the Republican-controlled Congress tried to end the war legally by a joint resolution, the President vetoed it. Wilson's successor, Warren Harding, and an enlarged Republican majority then agreed on a measure ending the war in July 1921. Lawmakers grew disillusioned with sending troops to participate in the occupation of Germany, however, and in 1923 the Senate passed a sense of the Senate resolution declaring that "the President should order the immediate return to the United States of all troops of the United States now stationed in Germany." The overwhelming vote, 57–6, including Democrats and Republicans and Versailles Treaty supporters and opponents, came just as the House Appropriations Committee was considering an amendment prohibiting any funds to maintain U.S. troops on the Rhine. Two days later, President Harding announced the withdrawal of the 1,000 soldiers.[5]

In February 1919, 2 days after Vice President Thomas Marshall cast the deciding vote to defeat a Senate resolution calling for U.S. troops to be withdrawn from their intervention in Soviet Russia, President Wilson ordered their withdrawal.[6]

World War II ended with the surrender of Germany and Japan, but the formal termination of the war did not come until 1951, when the Senate approved a peace treaty with Japan and Congress passed legislation formally ending the war with Germany. Fighting in Korea ended with an armistice in 1953. Direct American combat in the Vietnam War essentially ended with the Paris agreement in January 1973 and the return of prisoners of war in March. Congressional concerns about continued air operations in Cambodia, however, led to a formal law, accepted under duress by the Nixon administration, cutting off all funds for military operations in Southeast Asia as of August 15, 1973.

The 1991 Gulf War ended with the liberation of Kuwait and a ceasefire agreement between the commanding U.S. general and an Iraqi officer. U.S. combat deployments to Somalia ended in 1994 by an act of Congress accepting the Clinton administration's timetable for withdrawal. Peacekeeping operations in the Balkans continue to this day but with limited U.S. participation.

While formal congressional action has not been necessary to terminate U.S. involvement in major military operations in recent decades, the threat of such action has had an impact on policymakers. Although no President has accepted the War Powers Resolution as controlling on his actions, most of the post-1973 military combat operations that were not specifically authorized were essentially completed within the 90-day limit of that law.[7] In the case of Somalia, the United States withdrew offshore, turning the operation over to UN command until the deadly October 3 raid, which led to a promised and legislated withdrawal within 6 months. Even the three authorized wars—twice against Iraq and once in Afghanistan—accomplished their primary military missions, at least initially, within the 90-day window for combat. Thus, the inherent power of Congress to end a war has driven war planners to attempt to keep major combat operations short.

The historical record shows that Congress can force termination of a conflict earlier than the President might prefer, and that sometimes the mere threat of action, or nonbinding expressions of congressional sentiment, can be influential.

WAR AND POLITICS

In May 1918, Woodrow Wilson famously declared that "politics is adjourned" for the duration of the war. In fact, politics has never been adjourned during America's major military operations. War is a continuation of policy and politics by other means, so war aims and conduct must survive scrutiny by the political and policy processes established by law and custom (see table 6–2).

Despite their disdain for many political figures and cynicism about policymaking in Washington, many Americans still find it painful to think that political considerations influence decisions

Table 6–2. Examples of Political Factors Affecting Conflict

- Federalists and Republicans disagreed over the Quasi-War; President Adams distrusted Alexander Hamilton and tried to slow Hamilton's building of Army; Hamilton purged officer corps of Republicans.
- Federalists opposed War of 1812; Republicans saw political advantages in going to war.
- Democrats favored war with Mexico; many Whigs opposed it. Sectional disputes over the extension of slavery split Congress. President Polk's attempt to place a Democrat over Whig generals was blocked.
- Support in the North for restoring the Union was bipartisan, but disagreements over abolition and emancipation remained. Secretary of War Edwin Stanton arranged military deferrals to boost Republican vote in 1864 election.
- Democrats seized Cuban independence as a political issue even before President McKinley did; U.S. sugar producers forestalled annexation.
- President Wilson urged Democratic vote after declaring that "politics is adjourned" in 1918.
- President Franklin Roosevelt worked to ensure bipartisan support for prewar rearmament and aid to Europe, naming leading Republican interventionists to his cabinet.
- After initial support, Republican opposition to President Truman and the Korean War grew with the firing of General Douglas MacArthur and the military stalemate.
- Legislative activity against the war in Vietnam was subdued under President Johnson but grew under President Nixon; troop withdrawal announcements were timed for domestic political effect.
- Budget negotiators agreed to hold harmless Gulf War and savings and loan bailout funds in 1990; President George H.W. Bush waited until after 1990 elections to announce troop buildups for offensive operations.
- President Clinton was pressured to act in Haiti by the Congressional Black Caucus and southerners fearing an influx of refugees in 1994.
- President George W. Bush pressed Congress for a pre-election vote authorizing war against Iraq in 2002.

for or against war and about its conduct. With hallowed precedents like the two World Wars—the first to "end all wars" and make the world safe for democracy, the second to defeat fascism—Americans want to believe that all our wars are defensive, that they are launched only under extreme provocation, that the citizenry rally around the flag in support, and that no one should question the war or criticize its conduct—at least not before the troops come home and march in their victory parades. Americans also want to believe that decisions on warfighting are never tainted by political calculations.

Unfortunately, this belief is at variance with the historical record, and necessarily so. Wars are waged to achieve political objectives, even if those objectives are not always clearly stated or even sound. Decisions to prepare for war, whether in the abstract or in response to a perceived threat or opportunity, divert national resources and private wealth from intended uses, thereby engaging politicians and citizens in innumerable adjustments that raise political issues. The economic and other costs of actually waging war and the risks to national interests and values are weighed differently by citizens, which ensures disagreement within their government.

Disputes between the executive and legislative branches are frequent and well publicized, but the executive branch is not immune from internal disagreements. The President of the United States is the supreme American politician—elected in a national contest and constantly in the public eye—and is tempted to see himself as the only representative of all the people, or at least the only politician whose responsibility is to the entire Nation. But the President is advised by Cabinet and sub-Cabinet officials who usually hold their positions because of political considerations and the influence of political constituencies—and those officials often disagree among themselves, sometimes bitterly. Thus, the President's deliberations on strategic decisions are heavily influenced by political considerations from the beginning. Moreover, disputes often continue within the executive branch after the President has reached a decision. Even when a fundamental decision is accepted, implementation can be a cause of contention between and among civilian officials and military officers, and those disputes often find their way into congressional debates and hearings.

It is an inescapable fact that to sustain support for a war once begun and to get the substantial resources consumed by the conflict, Presidents must work hard to maintain political support for themselves and their policies. To some degree, that support can come directly from the people, but it is mediated by Congress, which often puts conditions on its support. Congress is a political institution whose Members must be responsive to public opinion in their constituencies and hence often disagree among themselves. While the President can impose—or attempt to impose—unity of effort on the executive branch, Congress exists in deliberate and permanent disunity—by party, by region, by institution, by differing electoral terms. It takes great effort to obtain majority support for any sustained and costly enterprise, such as a major military operation. It should not be surprising, therefore, when Members of Congress disagree with the President and his policies and impose their own political considerations in wartime. When operations become prolonged or stalemated, Members are inclined to demand change or else withdraw their support.

That war is a political act is evident from the fact that no President has sought or received authorization for a major military operation when one or both chambers of Congress was controlled by the opposition party, except for Eisenhower (Formosa and the Middle East), George H.W. Bush (Kuwait), and George W. Bush (after the 9/11 attacks and in Iraq). Eisenhower sought advance authorization for the use of force because he both believed the Constitution required interbranch collaboration and wanted to avoid a repeat of Korea, when Congress had not been required to commit to the operation. When Democrats insisted on a congressional role in the wars of the Bush presidencies, they wound up providing support.

Until the time of Franklin D. Roosevelt, U.S. Presidents tended to seek cooperation with Congress in advance of major military operations. Since then, however, except for Eisenhower and Lyndon Johnson, both of whom sought to avoid repeating the Korean precedent, Presidents have tried to deny Congress a role in warmaking while welcoming unsolicited support. Following are some of the other ways in which political considerations have affected the conduct of several of America's major military operations over the past two centuries.

The Quasi-War with France initially reflected a political division that had arisen in the Washington administration, when Jefferson and Madison and their political followers tended to side with France at the start of the French Revolution, while Hamilton and the Federalists saw U.S. interests as closer to those of Great Britain. The fight over the Jay Treaty with Britain led to local political organizations that became the cadres for the emerging political parties. When John Adams pressed for a military buildup to confront France, Jefferson and his followers resisted because they saw no real need to fight Europe's newest revolutionaries, and they did not want to create the military forces Adams requested.

Adams reported to lawmakers his receipt of discouraging messages from U.S. envoys sent to France, but it was the Republicans in Congress who demanded that he provide detailed documentation. Once the XYZ letters reached the legislators, they recognized that American honor had been challenged, and they responded with a frenzy of activity to build Armed Forces not only to protect U.S. interests on the high seas but also to defend against invasion with a sizable standing Army. Adams reached the high point of his Presidency, parading in military regalia to adoring crowds. For his annual address to Congress in December 1798, he had standing behind him the top Army officers chosen to lead the growing regiments, George Washington and Alexander Hamilton.

Political divisions among Federalists also affected the conduct of the war. Adams was so distrustful of Hamilton that he delayed for months the naming of officers for the enlarged Army and later decided on a surprise diplomatic initiative to end the conflict to keep Hamilton from achieving greater prominence and power. Hamilton, in turn, was determined to politicize the Army by naming only Federalists to senior positions.

The War of 1812 was spearheaded by the congressional War Hawks, mainly Republicans from the Nation's interior, who were fiercely resisted by New England Federalists, who benefited from trade and good relations with Britain. Madison also saw war as the best means to unify the Republican Party and to help his own reelection prospects in 1812.[8] Once war was declared, Congress was slow to provide the needed equipment because of disputes over the best means of financing the conflict. Who should be taxed is always a political issue, even when the purpose is to fight a war. Lawmakers reenacted the direct taxes and excises that had been used in the 1790s but still fell short and had to resort to significant borrowing.

The war with Mexico in 1846 reflected the declared goals of President Polk and the Democratic Party: to secure Texas, add California to the Union, and promote further westward expansion. The President provoked the war by sending General Zachary Taylor into disputed areas of Texas and then trumpeting the border clash in ways that forced skeptical Whigs to vote for the declaration of war. Although Polk had promised not to seek a second term, he was determined to minimize the Presidential prospects of his two senior generals, Taylor and Winfield Scott, both of whom were Federalists.

The Democrats and Whigs had contrasting views of the military. The Democrats tended to favor state militias and Federal volunteers and were highly suspicious of West Point and its products. The Whigs preferred the military professionals, who also tended to side with their party. General Scott complained that the President was seeking to undercut "every general who would not place [the] Democracy above God's country." Polk in turn confided to his diary that senior Army officers "are all Whigs and violent partisans."[9]

Congress was also divided politically and regionally, and those divisions affected its conduct during the war. House passage of the Wilmot Proviso to forbid slavery in any newly acquired territory led to a Senate filibuster of funds needed for the war. When Whigs gained control of the House after the 1846 elections, they began a series of antiwar measures, including an inflammatory amendment calling the war illegal (which narrowly passed the House) and other measures seeking confidential administration documents.[10]

The American Civil War was, of course, fundamentally a political dispute. With the resignation of southern Congressmen, President Lincoln faced a sympathetic Congress controlled by

Republicans and anti-slavery Democrats. He angered many of his supporters by giving Democrats high military rank. His slowness to embrace emancipation also upset the more radical Republicans, who pressed and voted for measures Lincoln resisted and had to veto. While he grew increasingly dissatisfied with the performance of his most prominent commander, General George McClellan, Lincoln waited until after the 1862 elections to fire him and was justifiably concerned about McClellan's political ambitions until the general's defeat in the 1864 elections. In the months before those elections, Secretary of War Edwin Stanton pressured military officers to help Republican state agents. Whole regiments were furloughed home to crucial states—where they voted overwhelmingly (78 percent) for Lincoln.[11] Nor is it surprising that Lincoln waited until after the apparent Union victory at Antietam in September 1862 to announce his emancipation plans.

The Spanish-American War was also profoundly political. Democrats pushed Cuban independence from their minority status in Congress, and President McKinley almost lost control of the issue. He had to accept a measure implicitly declaring war and issuing an ultimatum to Spain and then sought a second explicit declaration of war after Spanish rejection of the ultimatum. An important source of opposition to annexation of Cuba, which took the form of the Teller Amendment promising Cuba independence, was congressional delegations from states that produced cane or beet sugar. What to do about the Philippines also split Congress, largely on regional lines. The imperialists tended to come from coastal, seafaring, and trading areas, while the anti-imperialists were often from agricultural and interior states. Racial hostility also played a role in these political judgments.[12]

Several political conflicts affected World War I. President Wilson failed to get all of the rearmament measures he sought because of a Senate filibuster by a group of anti-interventionists. The infamous "little group of willful men" consisted mainly of progressive Republicans, mostly from the Midwest, and mainly southern Democrats hostile to Britain and its trade policies.[13]

Wilson then financed the war with a very progressive tax system that troubled conservatives. His decisions to impose price controls on wheat while allowing cotton prices to respond to the high market demand alienated wheat growing areas, mostly Republican, while keeping southern Democratic areas rich and happy. Republicans resisted approving conscription in the hope of allowing their former President, Theodore Roosevelt, to lead a corps of volunteers. The Democratic chairman of the Senate Military Affairs Committee became the most vocal critic of the administration's management of the war. Wilson infuriated Republicans by declaring, in May 1918, that "politics is adjourned" for the duration of the war, while later supporting sharp attacks against Republicans in the final days of the congressional election campaigns. In the final weeks of conflict before the November 11, 1918, armistice, Republicans pressed for unconditional surrender by Germany, while Wilson was willing to accept conditions consistent with his earlier Fourteen Points. And the leading opponent of the Versailles Peace Treaty, Senator Henry Cabot Lodge (R–MA), was so antipathetic to Wilson that he used every available means to undercut the President.

Perhaps the best example of a President who felt constrained by law in some areas but acted boldly in others was Franklin D. Roosevelt prior to Pearl Harbor. He sought and fought for revisions in the Neutrality Acts that prohibited arms sales to warring states and for Lend-Lease to provide weaponry to Britain, yet he forced his military leaders to sign off on the dubious legal rationale for the destroyer-for-bases deal and ordered military actions in the North Atlantic that clearly provoked Germany and resulted in attacks on U.S. ships. Fortunately for Roosevelt, he had a friendly Democratic Congress and strong support from the internationalist wing of the Republican Party. He also formed a bipartisan coalition in favor of helping Europeans threatened by Hitler. Isolationist opposition vanished after December 7, 1941, and there was extraordinary political unity during the war. Roosevelt did press his military commanders, who doubted the value and urgency of the mission, to launch attacks against German forces in North Africa before the 1942 congressional elections in order to help sustain public support for fighting Hitler first. And his announcement early in 1943 of a demand for unconditional surrender preempted domestic fights over war aims.

Despite initial unity over fighting aggression in Korea,

political fights soon emerged over the role of the Chinese Nationalists and whether to strike targets within China. General Douglas
MacArthur openly communicated with Republican leaders in Congress, airing his policy views and his criticisms of his Commander
in Chief. Truman's firing of the general led to a surge of support
for MacArthur and the collapse of Truman's own public approval.
Only the deft handling of the Senate hearings by Richard Russell
(D–GA) rescued Truman and his policy.

The Vietnam War began with broad bipartisan support but
ultimately ended with strong bipartisan opposition. In the early
years, Democrats in Congress held their fire despite growing un-
happiness with the war policy. Only with the election of Richard
Nixon and majority public opposition to the war did Congress actually try to legislate restrictions on the Nixon policies. Congress
found its greatest unity in measures prompted by the war but not
directly affecting it, such as the War Powers Resolution for future
wars and the National Commitments Resolution demanding more
information for Congress.

Political considerations affected the Gulf War as well. The
conflict broke out in late summer 1990 at precisely the time of
major budget negotiations in which the level of defense spending
was a key item. Administration and congressional negotiators decided to "hold harmless" funds related to the crisis, as well as to
the looming savings and loan bailout. When President George H.
W. Bush decided to send troops for offensive operations, he delayed his announcement until after the 1990 congressional elections. Many Democrats opposed immediate resort to combat in votes
that haunted many of them in the 1992 and subsequent elections.

President Bush waited until after the 1992 elections to decide to send U.S. troops into Somalia and then stated that their
mission would be concluded by the date of the inauguration of
President Clinton. After the ignominious withdrawal of U.S. troops
a year later, the Clinton administration felt politically constrained
not to intervene to stop the Rwandan genocide. Meanwhile, an
important plank in the Republican "contract with America" in the
1994 congressional campaign was to avoid the problems that had
beset the Clinton administration's military operations. On the other
hand, intervention in Haiti had strong domestic political support

from both the Congressional Black Caucus and Gulf Coast residents who feared an influx of Haitian refugees.

President George W. Bush obtained congressional authorization for attacks against Iraq by pressing for action before the 2002 elections and by agreeing to the only two demands made by congressional skeptics—seeking UN action and a vote by Congress. He also co-opted the House Democratic leader and thereby headed off bipartisan efforts under way in the Senate to restrict his plans.

While Presidents and lawmakers may pretend that their actions are not influenced by political considerations, such claims are not credible. Some political leaders may subordinate or even try to ignore political factors, but others will have incentives to respond to them.

LESSONS FROM THE PRECEDENTS

Congress at war is not a pretty sight. The legislative branch can be questioning and judgmental, impatient for victories yet free with inexpert advice, slow to provide the men and materiel for combat, reluctant to vote the taxes needed to pay for the war, critical of generals, and careless with secrets. But the legislative branch can also be submissive and deferential toward commanders from the President on down, uncritical and unquestioning despite evident problems, eager to avoid responsibility for its own action or inaction, and more concerned with domestic politics and economic policies than with the long-term health of the economy and the success of the troops.

The historical record shows that Congress can act, and has acted, in all of these ways. Despite widespread views that the standard—and preferred—practice is for Congress to go on vacation once a war starts, leaving all key decisions to the President and his commanders, there are ample precedents showing vigorous congressional involvement in the management and oversight of major military operations. Sometimes that involvement has been disruptive or even harmful, but often it has been constructive.

In recent years, Congress has tried—without much success—to mandate prior congressional approval of particular anticipated military operations, such as in Haiti, Bosnia, and Kosovo. Perhaps it is impossible to force reluctant Presidents to consult with Congress or to heed its demands for prior approval of anticipated military operations, even with mandatory language. The executive branch always has many excuses and legal arguments to avoid such steps. The alternative could be for Congress to resort more to substantive requirements and prohibitions instead of the procedural ones most common now.

The bottom line is that Congress need not sit on the sidelines as wars approach or are fought. The precedents listed here provide an ample menu of options, if lawmakers are willing to make the judgments and take the risks and opportunities available.

NOTES

Chapter 1: Introduction

1   Louis Smith, *American Democracy and Military Power* (Chicago: University of Chicago Press, 1951), 181.

2   Quoted in Peter J. Kastor, "Toward the Maritime War Only: The Question of Naval Mobilization, 1811–1812," *Journal of Military History* 61, no. 3 (July 1997), 474.

3   John Yoo, *The Powers of War and Peace* (Chicago: University of Chicago Press, 2006), 8.

4   Office of Legal Counsel, U.S. Department of Justice, "Memorandum for Alberto R. Gonzales," August 1, 2002, 33.

5   David B. Rivkin, Jr., and Lee A. Casey, "Constitutional Warp," *The Wall Street Journal*, January 31, 2007.

6   Robert F. Turner, *Repealing the War Powers Resolution* (Washington, DC: Brassey's, 1991), 81, 93.

7   Jane E. Stromseth, "Review: Understanding Constitutional War Powers Today: Why Methodology Matters," *Yale Law Journal* 106, no. 3 (December 1996), 879–880.

8   Christopher Collier and James Lincoln Collier, *Decision in Philadelphia: The Constitutional Convention of 1787* (New York: Ballantine Books, 1986), 123.

9   Ibid., 172–173, 248.

10 Richard H. Kohn, ed., *The U.S. Military Under the Constitution, 1789–1989* (New York: New York University Press, 1991), 71.

11 Collier and Collier, 323–329.

12 Ibid., 330–331.

13 Richard H. Kohn, *Eagle and Sword: The Beginnings of the Military Establishment in America* (New York: Free Press, 1975), 85–86.

14 Ibid., 97, 110–111, 120–123.

15 Ibid., 134–135.

16 The Framers chose slightly different language for seagoing forces—

to "provide and maintain a navy"—in recognition of the need to have warships in being in advance of conflicts.

Chapter 2: Declaration of War

1   David M. Ackerman and Richard F. Grimmett, "Declarations of War and Authorizations for the Use of Military Force: Historical Background and Legal Implications," Congressional Research Service Report for Congress, January 14, 2003.
2   U.S. Statutes at Large, Ch. 102, 2 Stat. 755.
3   Ch. 16, 9 Stat. 9.
4   30 Stat. 738; 30 Stat. 364.
5   Ch. 1, 40 Stat. 1.
6   Thomas W. Ryley, *A Little Group of Willful Men* (Port Washington, NY: Kennikat Press, 1975), 95, 5.
7   Ch. 561, 55 Stat. 795, Ch. 564, 55 Stat. 796, Ch. 565, 55 Stat. 797; and Chs. 323–325, 56 Stat. 307.
8   Ch. 48, 2 Stat. 561, May 28, 1798.
9   Ch. 67, 2 Stat. 578.
10 Ch. 68, 2 Stat. 578.
11 Ch. 4, 1 Stat. 129.
12 Ch. 46, 1 Stat. 291.
13 Annals of Congress, March 1815, 439.
14 Ch. 90, 3 Stat. 230.
15 Article I, section 8.
16 Ch. 25, 12 Stat. 281.
17 87 Stat. 555.
18 Public Law 98–119, 97 Stat. 805, October 12, 1983. For the texts of the notes between the United States and Lebanon, see Department of State Bulletin, September 1982, 4.
19 P.L. 107–40, 115 Stat. 224, September 18, 2001.
20 Richard F. Grimmett, "Authorization for Use of Military Force in Response to the 9/11 Attacks (P.L. 107–40): Legislative History," Congressional Research Service Report for Congress, January 4, 2006.
21 38 Stat. 770, April 20, 1914; John Whiteclay Chambers II, ed., *The Oxford Companion to American Military History* (New York: Oxford University Press, 1999), 432.
22 The vote was 87–1 in the Senate and 384–7 in the House. P.L. 87–733.
23 P.L. 88–408, 78 Stat. 384, August 10, 1964.
24 Robert David Johnson, *Congress and the Cold War* (Cambridge: Cambridge University Press, 2006), 117–118.
25 11 Stat. 370.
26 P.L. 84–4, Ch. 4, 69 Stat. 7, January 29, 1955.

27 Press Conference, April 4, 1956.
28 P.L. 85–7, 71 Stat. 5, March 9, 1957.
29 P.L. 102–1, 105 Stat. 3, January 14, 1991.
30 Jennifer K. Elsea and Richard F. Grimmett, "Declarations of War and Authorizations for the Use of Military Force: Historical Background and Legal Implications," Congressional Research Service Report for Congress, August 11, 2006, 15n.
31 P.L. 107–243, 116 Stat. 1498, October 16, 2002.
32 Max Boot, *The Savage Wars of Peace: Small Wars and the Rise of American Power* (New York: Basic Books, 2002), 125.
33 Russell F. Weigley, *History of the United States Army*, enlarged edition (Bloomington: Indiana University Press, 1984), 308; 30 Stat. 977.
34 John S.D. Eisenhower, *Intervention! The United States and the Mexican Revolution, 1913–1917* (New York: W.W. Norton, 1993), 281–282, 335; "President's Action Endorsed in Senate," *The New York Times*, March 18, 1916.
35 For discussion and sources, see Charles A. Stevenson, *Warriors and Politicians: U.S. Civil-Military Relations under Stress* (London: Routledge, 2006), 127–129.
36 Truman Presidential Museum and Library, Public Papers and Korean War Documents, at <www.trumanlibrary.org>; Foreign Relations of the United States, 1950, vol. VII: *Korea, Foreign Economic Policy* [FRUS 1950] (Washington, DC: Government Printing Office, 1976), 286–291.
37 *Congress and the Nation*, vol. II, 1965–1968 (Washington, DC: Congressional Quarterly Press, 1969), 66, 77.
38 Grimmett, "War Powers," 22.
39 Ibid., 30–31.
40 Ibid., 32.
41 Sect. 8147 of P.L. 103–139, Grimmett, "War Powers," 42.
42 P.L. 103–423; Grimmett, "War Powers," 43–44.
43 *Congress and the Nation*, vol. IX, 1993–1996 (Washington, DC: Congressional Quarterly Press, 1998), 225–228; Ivo Daalder, *Getting to Dayton* (Washington, DC: Brookings Institution, 2000), 61–64.
44 Grimmett, "War Powers," 38.
45 Ibid., 39–41.
46 U.S. Department of State, *Peace and War: United States Foreign Policy, 1931–1941* (Washington, DC: Government Printing Office, 1943), 23, 25, document 49.
47 *Peace and War*, 35, 37, documents 68, 83.
48 Hadley Cantril, *Public Opinion, 1936–1946* (Princeton: Princeton University Press, 1951), 967; Robert Dallek, *Franklin D. Roosevelt*

and American Foreign Policy, 1932–1945 (New York: Oxford University Press, 1995), 204; sect 14(a), 54 Stat. 681; Robert Shogan, *Hard Bargain* (New York: Scribner, 1995), 219.

49   50 U.S.C. App. 454.

50   James M. Lindsay, *Congress and the Politics of U.S. Foreign Policy* (Baltimore: The Johns Hopkins University Press, 1994), 84, 128; Louis Fisher, *Presidential War Power* (Lawrence: University Press of Kansas, 2ᵈ edition, revised, 2004), 137–139, 144–148, 246.

51   *Congress and the Nation*, vol. III, 1969–1972 (Washington, DC: Congressional Quarterly Press, 1973), 944; *Congress and the Nation*, vol. VII, 1985–1988 (Washington, DC: Congressional Quarterly Press, 1989), 216; Richard F. Grimmett, "Congressional Use of Funding Cutoffs since 1970 Involving U.S. Military Forces and Overseas Deployments," Congressional Research Service Report for Congress, January 16, 2007, 6; Juan Forero, "Congress approves doubling U.S. troops in Colombia," *The New York Times*, October 11, 2004.

52   See Lisa Mages, "U.S. Armed Forces Abroad: Selected Congressional Roll Call Votes Since 1982," Congressional Research Service Report for Congress, January 27, 2006; Amy Belasco et al., "Congressional Restrictions on U.S. Military Operations in Vietnam, Cambodia, Laos, Somalia, and Kosovo: Funding and Non-Funding Approaches," Congressional Research Service Report for Congress, January 16, 2007.

Chapter 3: Raise and Support Armies/Make Rules Governing Conduct

1   Howard White, "Executive Influence in Determining Military Policy in the United States," *University of Illinois Studies in the Social Sciences*, parts I and II, vol. XII, no. 1 (March 1924); 155, 155n; Ch. 47, 2 Stat. 558, May 28, 1798.

2   Ch. 766, 2 Stat. 604, July 16, 1798.

3   White, "Executive Influence," 173–175, 181; Weigley, *Army*, 118; Ch. 14, 2 Stat. 671, January 11, 1812; Ch. 53, 2 Stat. 704, April 8, 1812.

4   Ch. 15, 9 Stat. 9, May 13, 1846; Ch. 2, 2 Stat. 117, January12, 1847; Ch. 8, 9 Stat. 123, February 11, 1847; Ch. 61, 9 Stat. 184, March 3, 1847.

5   Ch. 9, 12 Stat. 269, July 22, 1861.

6   Ch. 191, 55ᵗʰ Cong, 2ᵈ sess., 30 Stat. 364, April 26, 1898.

7   Ch. 75, 12 Stat. 731, March 3, 1863; Ch. 13, Stat. 6, February 24, 1864; Weigley, *Army*, 210.

8   Chambers, 180–182; Seward W. Livermore, *Woodrow Wilson and the War Congress, 1916–18* (Seattle: University of Washington Press, 1966), 24–29.

9   See Stevenson, *Warriors and Politicians*, 104, 107–108; Chambers, 181.

10 50 U.S.C. App. 454.

11 *Congress and the Nation*, vol. III, 1969–1972 (Washington, DC: Congressional Quarterly Press, 1973), 229–231.

12 Article II, sect. 4.

13 See Stevenson, *Warriors and Politicians*, 90–91.

14 John H. Schroeder, *Mr. Polk's War: American Opposition and Dissent, 1846–1848* (Madison: University of Wisconsin Press, 1973), 65.

15 See Stevenson, *Warriors and Politicians*, 38, 46.

16 Michael C. Desch, *Civilian Control of the Military* (Baltimore: The Johns Hopkins University Press, 1999), 136; Forrest C. Pogue, *George C. Marshall: Organizer of Victory, 1943–1945* (New York: Viking Press, 1973), 267.

17 Chambers, 749–751.

18 William B. Skelton, *An American Profession of Arms: The Army Officer Corps, 1784–1861* (Lawrence: University Press of Kansas, 1992), 63, 215.

19 Chambers, 749–753.

20 Harold and Margaret Sprout, *The Rise of American Naval Power, 1776–1918* (Princeton: Princeton University Press, 1944), 33–35.

21 Leonard D. White, *The Federalists* (New York: Free Press, 1948), 160.

22 Kastor, 473; Donald R. Hickey, *The War of 1812* (Urbana: University of Illinois Press, 1990), 113.

23 Ch. 26, 2 Stat. 682, February 21, 1812; Chs. 25 and 26, 2 Stat. 105, March 19, 1814.

24 Ch. 95, 9 Stat. 68.

25 Weigley, *Army*, 219; no. 27, 12 Stat. 617 (April 10, 1862); Ch. 251, 13 Stat. 392, July 4, 1864.

26 Howard White, 227.

27 Weigley, *Army*, 348–350; Sprout and Sprout, 345.

28 Louis Fisher, *Presidential Spending Power* (Princeton: Princeton University Press, 1975), 240–244.

29 See HR 5631, DOD Appropriations Act, 2007.

30 Alexander DeConde, *The Quasi-War* (New York: Scribner's, 1966), 102; Ch. 75, 1 Stat. 597, July 14, 1798.

31 Ch. 46, 2 Stat. 291, March 26, 1804.

32 Claudia D. Goldin, "War," *Encyclopedia of American Economic History* (New York: Scribner's, 1980), 942.

33 Goldin, 938; Paul Studenski and Herman E. Krooss, *Financial History of the United States* (New York: McGraw-Hill, 1952), 150, 153.

34 Goldin, 938.

35 Ch. 448, 30 Stat. 448, June 13, 1898.
36 Goldin, 38; Studenski and Krooss, 297.
37 Livermore, 50.
38 Chambers, 577, 827; Goldin, 938.
39 Goldin, 938; Marc Labonte, "Financing Issues and Economic Effects of Past American Wars," Congressional Research Service Report for Congress, November 7, 2001, 7–8.
40 Labonte, 9–10.
41 Ibid., 13.
42 $549 thru FY07 plus $145B requested for FY08. Congressional Research Service and Office of Management and Budget.

Chapter 4: Strategy

1 Kastor, 460–461, 475–478; Hickey, 163.
2 Stevenson, *Warriors and Politicians*, 45–50.
3 Bruce Tap, *Over Lincoln's Shoulder: The Committee on the Conduct of the War* (Lawrence: University Press of Kansas, 1998), 102–104.
4 Hadley Cantril, "Opinion Trends in World War II: Some Guides to Interpretation," *Public Opinion Quarterly* 12, no. 1 (Spring 1948), 39; Roland Young, *Congressional Politics in the Second World War* (New York: Columbia University Press, 1956), 153; Pogue, *Organizer*, 197.
5 Richard E. Neustadt, *Presidential Power and the Modern Presidents* (New York: Free Press, 1990), 103–119.
6 David Hoffman, "Reagan Likely to Retain Limit of 55 on Trainers," *The Washington Post*, August 18, 1983; Juan Forero, "Congress Approves Doubling U.S. Troops in Colombia," *The New York Times*, October 11, 2004.

Chapter 5: Oversight

1 Christopher J. Deering, "Alarms and Patrols: Legislative Oversight in Foreign and Defense Policy," in *Congress and the Politics of Foreign Policy*, ed. Colton C. Campbell, Nicol C. Rae, and John F. Stack, Jr., (Upper Saddle River, NJ: Prentice Hall, 2003), 112–113.
2 P.L. 79–601; Deering, 119.
3 Deering, 114–115.
4 Stevenson, *Warriors and Politicians*, 59–60.
5 American State Papers, *Military Affairs*, vol. 1:119–120, 132; *Naval Affairs*, vol. 1:34, 37; *Foreign Relations*, vol. 2:285, all available at <http://memory.loc.gov/ammem/amlaw/lawhome.html>.
6 Smith, 181, 179.
7 Ibid., 183–185; American State Papers, *Military Affairs*, vol. 1:524–599.

8 Smith, 190–193.

9 See Stevenson, *Warriors and Politicians*, 46–48; and Tap, throughout.

10 Tap, 44–45, 198–199, 232–233.

11 Weigley, *Army*, 310–311.

12 Stuart Creighton Miller, *"Benevolent Assimilation": The American Conquest of the Philippines, 1899–1903* (New Haven: Yale University Press, 1984), 213–217.

13 Smith, 207–210; Livermore, 52–57.

14 Young, 227; Donald H. Riddle, *The Truman Committee* (New Brunswick: Rutgers University Press, 1964), 9–11.

15 Quoted in Pogue, *Organizer*, 197.

16 Young, 145–147, 45–46.

17 The UNRRA was created by the wartime allies in 1943 to provide economic assistance to European nations after the war and to repatriate and assist the refugees who would come under Allied control.

18 Young, 175, 184–185, 187, 192–195.

19 Senate Armed Services Committee calendars, 81st and 82[d] Congresses. See also <http://www.ausa.org/webpub/ DeptArmyMagazine. nsf/ byid/CCRN-6CCS3P> and <http://www.army.mil/cmh-pg/books/ korea/truce/ch11.htm>.

20 Johnson, *Congress and the Cold War*, 120, 129–130, 137–138.

21 Stevenson, *Warriors and Politicians*, 68.

22 Ibid., 175–176.

23 Charles A. Stevenson, *SecDef: The Nearly Impossible Job of Secretary of Defense* (Washington, DC: Potomac Books, 2006), 99.

24 Ryan C. Hendrickson, *The Clinton Wars* (Nashville: Vanderbilt University Press, 2002), 162.

25 Bradley Graham and Charles Babington, "2 GOP Chairmen at Odds over Hill Abuse Hearings," *The Washington Post*, May 19, 2004.

Chapter 6: Termination

1 DeConde, 291–292.

2 Hickey, 296, 298.

3 Warren Zimmerman, *First Great Triumph: How Five Americans Made Their Country a World Power* (New York: Farrar, Straus and Giroux, 2002), 127; Richard E. Welch, Jr., *Response to Imperialism: The United States and the Philippine-American War, 1899–1902* (Chapel Hill: University of North Carolina Press, 1979), 18–19.

4 Boot, 249.

5 Messages and Papers of the Presidents, Woodrow Wilson, May 20, 1920, vol. XVI, 8849; George Rothwell Brown, "Senate Asks Recall of U.S. Rhine Army," *The Washington Post*, January 7, 1923.

6 Boot, 223.

7　See David P. Auerswald and Peter F. Cowhey, "Ballotbox Diplomacy: The War Powers Resolution and the Use of Force," *International Studies Quarterly* 41 (1997), 505–528. The Act requires the President to report to Congress whenever U.S. Armed Forces are introduced "into hostilities or into situations where imminent involvement in hostilities is clearly indicated by the circumstances." The forces are supposed to be withdrawn within 60 days unless Congress passes legislation authorizing the use of force. In case of "unavoidable military necessity," the President may have an extra 30 days to complete the withdrawal.

8　Hickey, 27.

9　Michael D. Pearlman, *Warmaking and American Democracy* (Lawrence: University Press of Kansas, 1999), 96–97.

10　Schroeder, 153–154.

11　Stevenson, *Warriors and Politicians*, 49–50.

12　John L. Offner, "McKinley and the Spanish-American War," *Presidential Studies Quarterly* 34, no. 1 (March 2004), 50–61; Paul S. Holbo, "Presidential Leadership in Foreign Affairs: William McKinley and the Turpie-Foraker Amendment," *American Historical Review* 72, no. 4. (July 1967), 1321–1335.

13　Ryley, 20–36.

BIBLIOGRAPHY

DOCUMENT COLLECTIONS

Annals of Congress, American State Papers, Congressional Globe, Senate and House Journals, Statutes at Large, Congressional Record (into the 1870s), available at <http://memory.loc.gov/ammem/amlaw/lawhome.html>.

BOOKS AND ARTICLES

Auerswald, David P. and Peter F. Cowhey. "Ballotbox Diplomacy: The War Powers Resolution and the Use of Force." *International Studies Quarterly* 41 (1997).

Belasco, Amy, et al. "Congressional Restrictions on U.S. Military Operations in Vietnam, Cambodia, Laos, Somalia, and Kosovo: Funding and Non-Funding Approaches." Congressional Research Service Report for Congress, January 16, 2007.

Boot, Max. *The Savage Wars of Peace: Small Wars and the Rise of American Power*. New York: Basic Books, 2002.

Byrd, Robert C. *The Senate: 1789–1989, Addresses on the History of the United States Senate*. Washington, DC: Government Printing Office, 1988.

Cantril, Hadley. "Opinion Trends in World War II: Some Guides to Interpretation." *Public Opinion Quarterly* 12, no. 1 (Spring 1948).

―――. *Public Opinion, 1936–1946*. Princeton: Princeton University Press, 1951.

Carman, Harry J., and Reinhard H. Luthin. *Lincoln and the Patronage*. New York: Columbia University Press, 1943.

Chambers II, John Whiteclay, ed. *The Oxford Companion to American Military History*. Oxford University Press, 1999.

Chernow, Ron. *Alexander Hamilton*. New York: Penguin Press, 2004.

Coffman, Edward M. *The Hilt of the Sword: The Career of Peyton C. March*. Milwaukee: University of Wisconsin Press, 1966.

Cohen, Eliot A. *Supreme Command: Soldiers, Statesmen, and Leadership in Wartime*. New York: Free Press, 2002.

Collier, Christopher, and James Lincoln Collier. *Decision in Philadelphia: The Constitutional Convention of 1787*. New York: Ballantine Books, 1986.

Congress and the Nation, 1945–1964. Washington, DC: Congressional Quarterly Press, 1965.

Congress and the Nation, vol. II: 1965–1968. Washington, DC: Congressional Quarterly Press, 1969.

Congress and the Nation, vol. III: 1969–1972. Washington, DC: Congressional Quarterly Press, 1973.

Congress and the Nation, vol. IV: 1973–1976. Washington, DC: Congressional Quarterly Press, 1977.

Congress and the Nation, vol. V: 1977–1980. Washington, DC: Congressional Quarterly Press, 1981.

Congress and the Nation, vol. VI: 1981–1984. Washington, DC: Congressional Quarterly Press, 1985.

Congress and the Nation, vol. VII: 1985–1988. Washington, DC: Congressional Quarterly Press, 1989.

Congress and the Nation, vol. VIII: 1989–1992. Washington, DC: Congressional Quarterly Press, 1993.

Congress and the Nation, vol. IX: 1993–1996. Washington, DC: Congressional Quarterly Press, 1998.

Congress and the Nation, vol. X: 1997–2001. Washington, DC: Congressional Quarterly Press, 2002.

Cook, James F. *Carl Vinson: Patriarch of the Armed Forces*. Macon, GA: Mercer University Press, 2004.

Currie, David P. *The Constitution in Congress: The Federalist Period, 1789–1801*. Chicago: University of Chicago Press, 1997.

Daalder, Ivo. *Getting to Dayton*. Washington, DC: Brookings Institution, 2000.

Dallek, Robert. *Franklin D. Roosevelt and American Foreign Policy, 1932–1945*. New York: Oxford University Press, 1995.

DeConde, Alexander. *The Quasi-War*. New York: Scribner's, 1966.

Deering, Christopher J. "Alarms and Patrols: Legislative Oversight in Foreign and Defense Policy." In *Congress and the Politics of Foreign Policy*, ed. Colton C. Campbell, Nicol C. Rae, and John F. Stack, Jr. Upper Saddle River, NJ: Prentice Hall, 2003.

Desch, Michael C. *Civilian Control of the Military*. Baltimore: The Johns Hopkins University Press, 1999.

Dimock, Marshall Edward. *Congressional Investigating Committees*. Baltimore: The Johns Hopkins Press, 1929.

Donald, David Herbert. *Lincoln.* New York: Simon and Schuster, 1995.

Eisenhower, John S.D. *Intervention! The United States and the Mexican Revolution, 1913–1917.* New York: W.W. Norton, 1993.

Elkins, Stanley, and Eric McKitrick. *The Age of Federalism.* New York: Oxford University Press, 1993.

Elsea, Jennifer K., and Richard F. Grimmett. "Declarations of War and Authorizations for the Use of Military Force: Historical Background and Legal Implications." Congressional Research Service Report for Congress, August 11, 2006.

Elsea, Jennifer K., and Thomas J. Nicola. "Congressional Authority to Limit U.S. Military Operations in Iraq." Congressional Research Service Report for Congress, January 29, 2007.

Fisher, Louis. *Presidential Spending Power.* Princeton: Princeton University Press, 1975.

———. *Presidential War Power*, 2^d ed., rev. Lawrence: University Press of Kansas, 2004.

Fite, Gilbert C. *Richard B. Russell, Jr. Senator from Georgia.* Chapel Hill: University of North Carolina Press, 2002.

Foreign Relations of the United States, 1949. Volume I: National Security Affairs, Foreign Economic Policy. Washington, DC: Government Printing Office, 1976.

Foreign Relations of the United States, 1950. Volume I: National Security Affairs, Foreign Economic Policy. Washington, DC: Government Printing Office, 1977.

Foreign Relations of the United States, 1950. Volume VII: Korea, Foreign Economic Policy. Washington, DC: Government Printing Office, 1976.

Fuller, John Douglas Pitts. *The Movement for the Acquisition of all Mexico*. Baltimore: The Johns Hopkins Press, 1936.

Gibbons, William Conrad. *The U.S. Government and the Vietnam War: Executive and Legislative Roles and Relationships*, part IV: July 1965–January 1968. Princeton: Princeton University Press, 1995.

Goldin, Claudia D. "War." *Encyclopedia of American Economic History*. New York: Scribner's, 1980.

Graham, Bradley, and Charles Babington. "2 GOP Chairmen at Odds over Hill Abuse Hearings." *The Washington Post*, May 19, 2004.

Greenfield, Kent Roberts. *American Strategy in World War II: A Reconsideration*. Malabar, FL: Robert E. Krieger Publishing Co., 1982.

Grimmett, Richard F. "Authorization for Use of Military Force in Response to the 9/11 Attacks (P.L. 107–40): Legislative History." Congressional Research Service Report for Congress, January 4, 2006.

——. "The War Powers Resolution After Thirty Years." Congressional Research Service Report for Congress, March 11, 2004.

——. "War Powers Resolution: Presidential Compliance." Congressional Research Service Report for Congress, July 14, 2006.

——. "Congressional Use of Funding Cutoffs since 1970 Involving U.S. Military Forces and Overseas Deployments." Congressional Research Service Report for Congress, January 16, 2007.

Hagan, Kenneth J. *This People's Navy: The Making of American Sea Power*. New York: Free Press, 1991.

Hallett, Brien. *The Lost Art of Declaring War*. Urbana: University of Illinois Press, 1998.

Hatzenbuehler, Ronald L., and Robert L. Ivie. *Congress Declares War: Rhetoric, Leadership, and Partisanship in the Early Republic.* Kent, OH: Kent State University Press, 1983.

Healy, David. *Drive to Hegemony: The United States in the Caribbean 1898–1917.* Madison: University of Wisconsin Press, 1988.

Hendrickson, Ryan C. *The Clinton Wars.* Nashville: Vanderbilt University Press, 2002.

Herring, Pendleton. *The Impact of War.* New York: Farrar and Rinehart, Inc., 1941.

Hickey, Donald R. *The War of 1812.* Urbana: University of Illinois Press, 1990.

Historical Statistics of the United States, Colonial Times to 1970. Washington, DC: Department of Commerce, 1975.

Holbo, Paul S. "Presidential Leadership in Foreign Affairs: William McKinley and the Turpie-Foraker Amendment." *American Historical Review* 72, no. 4 (July 1967).

Huntington, Samuel P. *The Soldier and the State.* Cambridge: Harvard University Press, 1957.

Huzar, Elias. *"The Purse and the Sword:" Control of the Army by Congress through Military Appropriations, 1933–1950.* Ithaca: Cornell University Press, 1950.

Jackson, Robert H. *That Man: An Insider's Portrait of Franklin D. Roosevelt.* New York: Oxford University Press, 2003.

Johnson, Robert David. *Congress and the Cold War.* Cambridge: Cambridge University Press, 2006.
Karnow, Stanley. *In Our Image: America's Empire in the Philippines.* New York: Random House, 1989.

————. *Vietnam: A History*. New York: Penguin Books, 1983.

Kastor, Peter J. "Toward 'the Maritime War Only'": The Question of Naval Mobilization, 1811–1812." *Journal of Military History* 61, no. 3 (July 1997).

Kennedy, David M. *Over Here: The First World War and American Society*. New York: Oxford University Press, 1980.

Kohn, Richard H. *Eagle and Sword: The Beginnings of the Military Establishment in America*. New York: Free Press, 1975.

————, ed. *The U.S. Military under the Constitution, 1789–1989*. New York: New York University Press, 1991.

Kriner, Douglas L. "Taming the Imperial Presidency: Congress, Presidents, and the Conduct of Military Operations." Ph.D. diss., Harvard University, 2006.

Labonte, Marc. "Financing Issues and Economic Effects of Past American Wars." Congressional Research Service Report for Congress, November 7, 2001.

Lambert, Frank. *The Barbary Wars: American Independence in the Atlantic World*. New York: Hill and Wang, 2005.

Lindsay, James M. *Congress and the Politics of U.S. Foreign Policy*. Baltimore: The Johns Hopkins University Press, 1994.

Livermore, Seward W. *Woodrow Wilson and the War Congress, 1916–18*. Seattle: University of Washington Press, 1966.

Locher III, James R. *Victory on the Potomac: The Goldwater-Nichols Act Unifies the Pentagon*. College Station: Texas A&M University Press, 2002.

Logevall, Fredrik. "The Vietnam War." In *The American Congress*, ed. Julian E. Zelizer. Boston: Houghton Mifflin, 2004.

Mages, Lisa. "U.S. Armed Forces Abroad: Selected Congressional Roll Call Votes Since 1982." Congressional Research Service Report for Congress, January 27, 2006.

May, Ernest R. *Imperial Democracy*. New York: Harper, 1973.

————, ed. *The Ultimate Decision: The President as Commander in Chief*. New York: George Braziller, 1960.

McPherson, James M. *Battle Cry of Freedom: The Civil War Era*. New York: Oxford University Press, 1988.

Miller, Stuart Creighton. *"Benevolent Assimilation:" The American Conquest of the Philippines, 1899–1903*. New Haven: Yale University Press, 1984.

Millis, Walter, ed. *The Forrestal Diaries*. New York: Viking, 1951.

Musicant, Ivan. *Banana Wars*. New York: Macmillan, 1990.

Neustadt, Richard E. *Presidential Power and the Modern Presidents*. New York: Free Press, 1990.

Office of Legal Counsel, U.S. Department of Justice. "Memorandum for Alberto R. Gonzales," August 1, 2002.

Offner, John L. "McKinley and the Spanish-American War," *Presidential Studies Quarterly* 34, no. 1 (March 2004), 50–61.

Paige, Glenn D. *The Korean Decision: June 24–30, 1950*. New York: Free Press, 1968.

Pearlman, Michael D. *Warmaking and American Democracy*. Lawrence: University Press of Kansas, 1999.

Pierson, William Whatley, Jr. "The Committee on the Conduct of the Civil War." *American Historical Review* 23, no. 3 (April 1918).

Pogue, Forrest C. *George C. Marshall: Ordeal and Hope, 1939–1942*. New York: Viking, 1966.

————. *George C. Marshall: Organizer of Victory, 1943–1945*. New York: Viking, 1973.

Ratner, Sidney. *American Taxation*. New York: W.W. Norton, 1942.

Riddle, Donald H. *The Truman Committee*. New Brunswick: Rutgers University Press, 1964.

Rivkin, David B., Jr., and Lee A. Casey. "Constitutional Warp." *The Wall Street Journal*, January 31, 2007.

Roosevelt, Franklin D. *The Public Papers and Addresses of Franklin D. Roosevelt, 1939*. New York: Macmillan, 1941.

————. *The Public Papers and Addresses of Franklin D. Roosevelt, 1940*. New York: Macmillan, 1941.

————. *The Public Papers and Addresses of Franklin D. Roosevelt, 1941*. New York: Harper and Brothers, 1950.

————. *Roosevelt's Foreign Policy, 1933–1941: Franklin D. Roosevelt's Unedited Speeches and Messages*. New York: Wilfred Funk, Inc., 1942.

Rosenman, Samuel I. *Working with Roosevelt*. New York: Harper and Brothers, 1952.

Ryley, Thomas W. *A Little Group of Willful Men*. Port Washington, NY: Kennikat Press, 1975.

Schmidt, Hans. *The United States Occupation of Haiti, 1915–1934*. New Brunswick: Rutgers University Press, 1995.

Schoonmaker, Herbert G. *Military Crisis Management: U.S. Intervention in the Dominican Republic, 1965*. New York: Greenwood Press, 1990.

Schroeder, John H. *Mr. Polk's War: American Opposition and Dissent, 1846–1848*. Madison: University of Wisconsin Press, 1973.

Seigenthaler, John. *James K. Polk*. New York: Henry Holt/Times Books, 2003.

Senate Select Committee on Haiti and Dominican Republic, "Inquiry into the Occupation and Administration of Haiti and Santo Domingo." 67th Cong., 1st and 2[d] sess., 1922.

Sherwood, Robert E. *Roosevelt and Hopkins*, rev. ed. New York: Universal Library, 1950.

Shogan, Robert. *Hard Bargain*. New York: Scribner, 1995.

Singletary, Otis A. *The Mexican War*. Chicago: University of Chicago Press, 1960.

Skelton, William B. "Officers and Politicians: The Origins of Army Politics in the United States before the Civil War." In *The Military in America*, ed. Peter Karsten. New York: The Free Press, 1986.

―――. *An American Profession of Arms: The Army Officer Corps, 1784–1861*. Lawrence: University Press of Kansas, 1992.

Skowronek, Stephen. *The Politics Presidents Make: Leadership from John Adams to George Bush*. Cambridge: Harvard University Press, 1993.

Smith, Louis. *American Democracy and Military Power*. Chicago: University of Chicago Press, 1951.

Smythe, Donald. "'Your Authority in France Will be Supreme': The Baker-Pershing Relationship in World War I." In Lloyd J. Matthews and Dale E. Brown, *The Parameters of War*. Washington, DC: Pergamon-Brassey's, 1987, 138–148.

Sofaer, Abraham D. *War, Foreign Affairs and Constitutional Power: The Origins.* Cambridge: Ballinger, 1976.

Solomon, Deborah. "How War's Expense Didn't Strain Economy." *The Wall Street Journal*, February 5, 2007.

Spanier, John W. *The Truman-MacArthur Controversy and the Korean War.* New York: Norton, 1965.

Sprout, Harold, and Margaret Sprout. *The Rise of American Naval Power, 1776–1918.* Princeton: Princeton University Press, 1944.

Stagg, J.C.A. *Mr. Madison's War.* Princeton: Princeton University Press, 1983.

Stevenson, Charles A. "The Evolving Clinton Doctrine on the Use of Force." *Armed Forces and Society* 22, no. 4 (Summer 1996).

———. *SecDef: The Nearly Impossible Job of Secretary of Defense.* Washington, DC: Potomac Books, 2006.

———. *Warriors and Politicians: U.S. Civil-Military Relations under Stress.* London: Routledge, 2006.

Stimson, Henry L., and McGeorge Bundy. *On Active Service in Peace and War.* New York: Harper and Brothers, 1948.

Stone, Geoffrey R. *Perilous Times: Free Speech in Wartime.* New York: W.W. Norton, 2004.

Stromseth, Jane E. "Review: Understanding Constitutional War Powers Today: Why Methodology Matters." *Yale Law Journal* 106, no. 3 (December 1996), 845–915.

Studenski, Paul, and Herman E. Krooss. *Financial History of the United States.* New York: McGraw-Hill, 1952.

Sullivan, Mark. *Our Times, 1900–1925*, vol. V, *Over Here, 1914–1918*. New York: Charles Scribner's Sons, 1972.

Tap, Bruce. *Over Lincoln's Shoulder: The Committee on the Conduct of the War*. Lawrence: University Press of Kansas, 1998.

Trefousse, H.L. *Benjamin Franklin Wade: Radical Republican from Ohio*. New York: Twayne Publishers, Inc., 1963.

Truman Presidential Museum and Library. Public Papers and Korean War Documents, available at <www.trumanlibrary.org>.

Turner, Robert F. *Repealing the War Powers Resolution*. Washington, DC: Brassey's, 1991.

U.S. Department of Commerce. *Historical Statistics of the United States: Colonial Times to 1970*. Washington, DC: Bureau of the Census, 1975.

U.S. Department of State. *Peace and War: United States Foreign Policy, 1931–1941*. Washington, DC: Government Printing Office, 1943.

U.S. Senate. Committee on Armed Services, 90th Cong., 1st sess., "Air War Against North Vietnam." Summary Report by Preparedness Investigating Subcommittee, August 31, 1967.

Watson, Mark Skinner. *Chief of Staff: Prewar Plans and Preparations*. Washington, DC: Historical Division, Department of the Army, 1950.

Weigley, Russell F. *History of the United States Army*, enlarged edition. Bloomington: Indiana University Press, 1984.

———. *The American Way of War*. Bloomington: Indiana University Press, 1977.

———. *A Great Civil War*. Bloomington: Indiana University Press, 2000.

Welch, Richard E., Jr. *Response to Imperialism: The United States and the Philippine-American War, 1899–1902*. Chapel Hill: University of North Carolina Press, 1979.

Westerfield, H. Bradford. *Foreign Policy and Party Politics: Pearl Harbor to Korea*. New Haven: Yale University Press, 1955.

White, Howard. "Executive Influence in Determining Military Policy in the United States." *University of Illinois Studies in the Social Sciences*, parts I and II, vol. XII, no. 1, March 1924.

White, Leonard D. *The Federalists*. New York: Free Press, 1948.

Williams, T. Harry. *Lincoln and the Radicals*. Madison: University of Wisconsin Press, 1965.

Woods, Jeff. *Richard B. Russell: Southern Nationalism and American Foreign Policy*. Lanham, MD: Rowman and Littlefield, 2006.

Woods, Randall Bennett. *Fulbright: A Biography*. Cambridge: Cambridge University Press, 1995.

Wormuth, Francis D., and Edwin B. Firmage. *To Chain the Dog of War*. Dallas: Southern Methodist University Press, 1986.

Yoo, John. *The Powers of War and Peace*. Chicago: University of Chicago Press, 2006.

Young, Roland. *Congressional Politics in the Second World War*. New York: Columbia University Press, 1956.

Zimmerman, Warren. *First Great Triumph: How Five Americans Made Their Country a World Power*. New York: Farrar, Straus and Giroux, 2002.

ABOUT THE AUTHOR

CHARLES A. STEVENSON, Ph.D., has served as a defense and foreign policy adviser in the U. S. Senate for 22 years. A long-time professor at the National War College in Washington, DC, he now teaches at the Nitze School of Advanced International Studies at The Johns Hopkins University. He lives in University Park, Maryland.